GOD COMES

TO AMERICA

FATHER DIVINE AND THE PEACE MISSION MOVEMENT

KENNETH E. BURNHAM

LAMBETH PRESS
BOSTON

Library of Congress Cataloging in Publication Data
Burnham, Kenneth E.
God comes to America.
Bibliography: p. 162.
Includes index.
1. Father Divine.
2. Peace Mission Movement.   3. Peace Mission
Movement—Biography.   I. Title.
BX7350.B87   301.5'8   78-27677
ISBN 0-931186-01-3

Contents

Preface:
A Note
on Research

The author first became interested in the Peace Mission Movement as a teacher and student of the sociology of religion. For many years he has taken his classes to visit services at the Circle Mission Church in Philadelphia, because they so well exemplified, in a fresh and even startling manner, concepts used in studying this subject.

In 1960 it was decided to do a serious study of the Movement, focusing on the charismatic aspect. The original intention was to interview as many as a hundred followers, but this soon turned out to be impractical. It became obvious that under intensive observation, a process which involved our attending meetings at all three churches in Philadelphia and two in New York City, the followers became very sensitive to outside judgments and wary of being misunderstood.

A second problem making interviews difficult was the separation of the sexes. Men do not converse with women in the member groups except on business, and then very minimally. Even informal talks with women were brief; after a few shy words they were gone. A female associate helped with some "semi-participant observation," which was useful. At banquets (communion meals), at restaurants, at praise meetings (worship services), in the limousines of the churches, in the hotels, and at Woodmont the sexes were always separated.

A third problem in meeting large numbers of followers arose from the custom of providing each "stranger" with a host. Furthermore, during the working day members were not at home or available for interviews. If they were not working, much of their time was consumed in Bible classes, New Day reading groups, Communion Banquets, administration of the churches, and religious services. They were found at leisure only at Woodmont on Saturday or Sunday afternoons.

A compromise arrived at for the author—to become a "semi-participant observer"—allowed him to attend Communion Banquets, services, Wedding Anniversary Celebrations (1960-1978), Woodmont Anniversary Celebrations (1961-1978) and to eat once or twice a week in the cafeterias of the Philadelphia churches or in the restaurants of the Hotel Lorraine or the Hotel Tracy. He attended Saturday and Sunday Communions (dinners) and Sunday services in the New York churches during 1961. Several Saturday and Sunday visits of many hours' duration were made to Woodmont from 1960 to the present.

Altogether at least fifty meetings and fifty Communions were observed between 1960 and 1977. At least a hundred different people were informally interviewed but only a few responded to long interrogations as originally planned.

For what the author considers a matter of professional ethics, nothing is quoted in the text which was not said in public as a testimony or printed in the various newspapers of the Movement. However, in the interviews a good deal was learned about attitudes and personal experiences.

It was soon apparent that the testimonies and even the accounts of individual experiences usually appeared verbatim in the *New Day*. (This could be verified by listening to the testimonies and speeches at any Communion service and then finding them printed just as they had been heard.) The writer found his own statements at a banquet accurately reproduced in the paper. This meant that the *New Day* is a reliable record of almost anything heard in public, representing the Movement's "definition of the situation," and a chronology of events.

A file of the *New Day* was available which gave a record of the Movement going back to 1931. In 1967 a file of all the different newspapers which, at one time or another, have printed verbatim talks of Father Divine was studied for three months.

The *New Day* prints forty-eight or more tabloid-size pages each week. The bulk of them, some twelve to twenty pages, are complete transcripts of sermons preached from 1931 on, printed and reprinted many times. Next in quantity, from one to five pages, are letters to Father Divine and their answers from him (after 1965 answered by Mother Divine). "Office Talks" (statements to his Secretaries) of Father Divine covering almost any topic, occupy a page or more in each issue. Often there is an interview with Father (and now Mother) by a seeker, a follower, a reporter, or a minister. Testimonies of physical, economic, or spiritual help often appear. (The issues of January, February, and March 1968 contain thirty-nine.) Last come news releases detailing developments in the areas of life to which Father Divine addressed himself: race relations, international amity, employment, population control, other religious groups' acceptance of his terminology or ideology of "positive thinking." These are seen as the working out of Father's intentions for the world. Accounts of retribution to those who resisted Father Divine's will are also set forth.

By following up the leads resulting from careful study of these original documents, the writer was able to orient himself to the Movement as he began attending meetings and visiting with its members. Thus data was accumulated, first by getting information from the paper, then verifying it by personal observation and talks with the followers. The *New Day,* in this student's opinion, gives a true picture of the Movement as seen by its participants.

The doctoral thesis[1] which resulted from the first three years of research became the basis of the new effort, namely, this book. Between 1963 and 1978 the author continued to visit, by himself and with students, and to read the *New Day.* Access was made available to the file of publications containing Father Divine's messages, and opportunity again provided to talk informally to many followers. Again, respect for the members' sincere and vital convictions posed problems in asking and getting answers to certain questions. In similar research, sociologists have documented such difficulties in interviewing leaders and followers in religious groups.[2]

A Note on Omissions

Throughout the manuscript the term *movement* has been used to refer to the accretion of members and the formation of formal church groups. This was, in part, a convenience in terminology, since, in the language of the followers and earlier books, it was the word used to refer to the collective activities of all the various groups and individuals influenced by Father Divine. Omitted from this book is any theoretical and analytical discussion of it as a sociological phenomenon or "social movement." Smelser in his *Theory of Collective Behavior*[3] presents Father Divine's activities and followers as an example of a "value-oriented social movement." Cantril, King, and others treat our topic as a social movement, but there is still room for a full, in-depth treatment of the Peace Mission Movement as a social-religious movement."[4]

Another omission, which may be painful to the professional sociologist of religion, has to do with the use of the concepts of "cult," "sect," and "denomination," or even the word *church* in the Troeltschian sense.[5] Here again, at least two of these terms (*cult* and *sect*) have been used in the sociological literature to refer to Father Divine's followers. An analysis of the group could well be done using these ideal-type constructs as, for instance, Wilson has done in comparing and contrasting Elim Tabernacle, Christian Science, and the Christadelphians in England.[6] But, hoping to interest the lay reader as well as the professional, the author felt that such an analysis could be confusing and is not essential to the task of understanding the charismatic aspects of Father Divine and the group.

Invocation

*Condescendingly I came as an existing Spirit
unembodied until condescendingly imputing
Myself in a Bodily Form in the likeness
of men I came, that I might speak to them
in their own language, coming to a country
that is supposed to be the Country of the
Free, where mankind has been privileged
to serve GOD according to the dictates of
his own conscience—coming sponsoring this
Peace Mission and this Spiritual revelation
in the hearts of the children of men, and
establishing the Kingdom of GOD in the
midst of them; that they might become to
be living epistles as individuals, seen and
read of men, and verifying that which has
long since been said!*

*The Tabernacle of GOD is with men,
and HE shall dwell with them, and
GOD HIMSELF shall be with them,
and shall be their GOD, and they shall
be HIS people!*

FATHER DIVINE

Preface to The Shrine at Woodmont, *published by the Peace Mission Movement*

I

From
Reverend
to
Father

*"What are the social conditions under which charismatic
leadership emerges and flowers and dies?"*

Charles Y. Glock

Father Divine's Peace Mission Movement which emerged in the depression of
the 1930s survives and continues today with enthusiastic, organized groups of
followers who live by his teachings. Concentrated around New York, Philadelphia,
and New Jersey, the membership spreads farther to Canada, California, and
around the globe. Although Father Divine is now dead as the world understands
such things, to his followers he is still very much alive, for to them he was not only
endowed as a man with supernatural qualities, but he was and *is* God.[1] In their
view, all acts credited to God throughout history were acts of Father Divine.

The Rev. M. J. Divine, as he was known before the Movement grew to prominence, is a prime subject for the study of charisma, a term implying complete
faith in a leader's supernatural qualities. The sociologist C. Wendell King wrote:

> In the person of Father Divine is found as close a resemblance to the charis-
> matic type as most mortals could aspire to. If his power is not absolute, it is
> very nearly so; if his personality has not molded the entire movement, the
> marks it has left are prominent and distinctive. His identification as God
> and his followers' belief in his physical immortality are added evidence of
> the charisma which resides in him.[2]

The aspect to be stressed particularly in this study is the function of Father Divine's
charismatic nature in providing a form and structure for the Peace Mission Movement.

What compels people to sever their affiliations with other religious groups, leave
their families, enter new occupations, and establish new residences in order to
become a part of the Peace Mission Movement? "What are the social conditions
under which charismatic leadership emerges and flowers and dies?"[3] These questions may be answered in part by examining the impact of Father Divine and his
close circle of followers on thousands of individuals from many countries and var-

ious ethnic and "racial" groups—many of whom significantly altered their lives
to create a new heaven and a new earth under the "Godhead" of Father Divine.

The charismatic leader is a recurrent figure in the literature of religious sects and
movements. The word *charisma,* borrowed from the New Testament Greek word
meaning "gift of grace," was given its sociological meaning by Max Weber.

> It is a certain quality of an individual personality by virtue of which he is set
> apart from ordinary men and treated as endowed with supernatural, super-
> human, or at least specifically exceptional powers or qualities. These are
> such as are not accessible to the ordinary person, but are regarded as of divine
> origin or as exemplary, and on the basis of them the individual concerned is
> treated as a leader.[4]

Weber suggests that any ethical, aesthetic, or more objective judgment of a charismatic individual's extraordinary quality is irrelevant to his definition. How the
leader is actually regarded by his followers and disciples constitutes the whole
significance of his charisma. They accept his leadership solely because of an awe-
some personal "power" sometimes credited to supernatural sources and validated
in successful performance, similar to the "mana" or "orenda" of anthropological
literature.[5]

Weber hypothesizes that "the source of their faith is the 'proving' of the charismatic quality through miracles, through victories and other successes, that is
through the welfare of the governed."[6] Psychologically this results in complete
personal devotion to the charismatic figure—whether it arises from enthusiasm
or despair and hope.

Accepting this meaning and this explanation of the social and psychological
sources of his power, we can describe Father Divine's actions in terms of what
they meant to his followers and to himself.

A number of studies by sociologists and anthropologists, of groups variously
called cults and sects, have utilized standard sociological concepts, but few have
focused on the role of the charismatic leader.[7]

The body of Major Jealous Divine, better known as Father Divine, lies in a $300,000
shrine on an estate in an exclusive suburb of Philadelphia. Next to the shrine is a
thirty-room stone mansion surrounded by seventy-three acres of forest, lawn,
and gardens. Here Mother Divine and her staff entertain followers of Father
Divine who come from all over the world to be close to "the Body." They believe
the spirit that was in his body is still present and as "operative as it ever was."

At Sayville, Long Island, there is another shrine—a wooden house on a small lot on a small street, where the leader first attracted followers in the 1920s. The change of ambience from Sayville to the estate in the Philadelphia suburbs is the story of Major J. Divine's transformation to Father Divine, and his acquisition of charisma.

There is no clear trace of the existence of Major Jealous Divine before 1914. When he was questioned about his place of birth, time of birth, or early history, his answers were always ambiguous. Although his followers accept June 6, 1882, as the date of his first marriage, a legal document in the courthouse at Mineola, New York, states that he was born in Providence, Rhode Island in 1880. In an interview in 1932 he said his age was around fifty-two "according to the legal records, but we have spiritually and mentally no record."[8]

In the 1930s, when he became a controversial figure, with his arrest, release, investigation, and attendant publicity, it was claimed that M. J. Divine was not his original name. He responded, "I have been called many things, I have been called by many names, but not the one that you are now claiming I used."

Speaking of himself in the third person he explained at a later date:

> He once had an old name, but when he was given a new name and those that would handle it and try to apply it to him, they were cursed and went down like Judge Smith did. It is wonderful. And, like many others have when they try to refute the Word of God, the works of the Almighty. Who can defile the Army of the living God? . . . some [people] shall not taste death until they see Me manifested in My Glory.[9]

Father Divine held that focusing on his personal saga would interfere with his followers' spiritual rebirth and with his own mission. He urged that his followers shed their old identities as well.

> You should be dead as a person, so that the Spirit of God's Presence might work for you and through you.
>
> That is why you did not hear anything about Me until a few years ago. When Moses was born, they did not hear anything about him, did they? It is indeed wonderful! He was hid in the ark of the bull-rushes, that he might not be seen and heard until the time he had grown to be too large for the ark. This is the mystery of the Spirit—losing your identity.
>
> You have not heard Me mention a Personal expression in the way of education and any pedigree, for the purpose of establishing Myself, but to the contrary. I have striven to hide, if possible, every expression that would tend to reflect mortality, or human's intelligence other than that which I

bring forth by My Spirit, through God's Omniscience within Me, of Whom you say I am.[10]

The emphasis on a new spiritual person, on turning from a past identity to a new one, has been a persistent theme in the Movement. Father Divine countered questions about his past existence with assertions of his spiritual continuum with God. Many followers have taken new names to express their sense of having entered into a new spiritual life. References to the past would be made only for comparison with what the new life has accomplished in overcoming past sin and suffering.

Popular writers' attempts to reconstruct Father Divine's unrecorded earlier years cannot be verified and, for the purposes of this study, they need not be. Until someone recognizes his extraordinary power, the charismatic figure is powerless, unless he happens to occupy a position in a group that gives him authority. This distinction between the power secured from a position of authority and the power an individual exerts through his followers' faith in his ordinary or supernatural powers is what Weber identified by the term *charisma*.

According to Weber, "domination" (what here has been called authority) comes in three distinct forms:[11] legal, traditional, and charismatic. Legal authority "rests upon rules that are rationally established by enactment, by agreement, or by imposition." The official is anyone who holds the power of command given him "as a trustee of the impersonal and 'compulsory institution'"; but he has this power only because of his position in the group, not because of his personality. "The 'area of jurisdiction' is a functionally delimited realm of possible objects of command and thus delimits the sphere of the official's legitimate power." Officials and members of an association may appeal or complain to a hierarchy of superiors. Over a period of time rules develop to which both officials and citizens or members must give heed. Power, domination, or authority is vested not in the individual but in his position and its relationship to other positions.

Traditional authority, according to Weber, is based on long established inherited status The possessors of this power are *masters,* to whom *followers* or *subjects* give personal loyalty and obedience out of pious respect for their time-honored position. Patrimonial and feudal societies manifest this form of domination.

In contrast to either legal or traditional authority, charismatic leadership rests on the status one man has achieved by extraordinary signs of his having supernatural powers: through revelations made known to him, heroic feats he has performed, or remarkable events that have distinguished his rise to prominence. Those who accept such leadership are disciples or followers; they obey their leader for his rare personal qualities rather than for any rule in established business, political, or religious organizations. They are not concerned that he be a member of the traditional ruling group, having rejected both legal and traditional domination.

This excursion into theory may give new meaning to Father Divine's insistence that his history as an ordinary human being was of no importance. He occupied no position of power in an already accepted group, was not a business owner or administrator in the usual sense, or a political leader; he was not an ordained representative of any organized religious group, nor was he a member of a powerful social class. As he said, "You have not heard me mention a personal expression in the way of education and any human pedigree, for the purpose of establishing myself," indicating that his authority was entirely charismatic, reflected in the attitude of his followers who ascribed to him more than human intelligence.

> I have striven to hide, if possible, every expression that would tend to reflect mortality, or human's intelligence other than that which I bring forth by My Spirit, through God's Omniscience within Me, of Whom you say I am.

Father Divine apparently had been an itinerant preacher before settling down in a home in Sayville, Long Island, in 1919. He claimed no formal education, nor ordination by any religious group. He identified with the segment of the population which had been enslaved and still suffered great indignities. He held that much of the legal action taken against him stemmed from the unconstitutional practice of racial discrimination. His characteristic manner of speech and appearance he explained as God's way of reaching people who needed to hear God, who were not being reached by ordinary preachers.

He recalled that no one really knew who he was when he came to Sayville. His wife, Peninah, bought the house with her earnings, but it became home to many followers through the years. Individuals came to ask spiritual advice of Major Divine. Some began to call him Father because they felt he had helped them to become "born again." They were the spiritual children of Father Divine. With his help some found work in the area; others helped around "home." The Reverend Father Divine became the center of existence for many of them. They asked his advice and communed with him at his dinner table. He satisfied both their spiritual and their material needs. As they traveled about they told others of their experiences.

Three popular books[12] have tried to piece together accounts of Major Jealous Divine's earlier life, but neither he nor his followers accepted them as true.

Father Divine's personal account of his thoughts and actions during the move to Sayville has become part of the literature of the Movement. To the true believer it is an adequate explanation of the inception of Father Divine's great work. (Frequent use of capital letters is typical of the Movement's printed material):

> I decided in 1914 . . . or just before that time to try to Personally refrain from coming into contact, and running into collision with the other versions of GOD and other religions. So when I moved out on Long Island, I said, "I do not want anything out here in Sayville, but MY Own Unadulterated MIND, MY Own Spirit, and MY Own LIFE and MY Own Unadulterated LOVE." Hence we remained out there and I decided to give practical service to humanity, at that time, by giving men work, blessing them with positions, etc. and only appearing from time to time among the people, as any other ordinary Preacher. . . . I had gone into Mental and Spiritual Seclusion, that I might not be observed by the different Religions to conflict them, for MY very PRESENCE WITH MY VERSION is conflicting to the different Religions.

> "I will do GOOD in that way . . . and I will run a Free Employment Agency . . . place help wheresoever a person wants help. I will place help with them *free* of charge—the RICH, the poor and all, MY SERVICE will be as a GIFT OF GOD." And so I did, but seeing many in need, eventually the people began to learn. They began to learn of ME, from time to time coming out one after the other.[13]

All attempts to describe Father Divine's history have been rejected by his followers on the ground that his life can be understood only from his own words in the publications of the Movement. They believe that the only true statements about him have come from his own lips.

John DeVoute, editor for more than thirty years of the *New Day,* answered a query from a professor of theology in 1961 about the use of other sources than those endorsed by Father Divine:

> We have taken the time to extract excerpts that, we hope, will give you a true picture of Father Divine from His own Words. . . . This has been compiled hurriedly and much real information has been omitted that should be included to give a glimpse of the reality of Father's Work.

> The New Day Publishing Company is an independent commercial enterprise to which Father Divine has contributed gratis for many years those of His Sermons, Letters, and Office Talks released for publication. Having close, personal contact with Father Divine for such a long time, we are in a position to know that the books from which your institution has taken its material for study could not be less factual. Much of the fabrication is cut

from whole cloth without a thread of truth. . . . None of the authors listed has had any close or personal association with Father Divine or the Peace Mission Movement. It is obvious that an attempt has been made in each instance to capitalize on His Name without the slightest regard or consideration for His Purpose.

The material we are submitting to you has been taken mostly from our own files for convenience. Father's Messages and Sermons were published long before the *New Day* or *Spoken Word* carried them. An examination of such publications as the *Light*, the *Divine Light*, the *Metaphysical News*, the *New York News*, the *Voice*, the *World Herald*, the *World Echo*, etc.[14] reveals the consistency of Father Divine's Doctrine. The truth of Father's Work and Mission was available long before any of the books listed in your bibliography were published. The failure of the authors to convey the truth was undoubtedly an intentional attempt to cast a shadow of doubt, ignorance and superstition over his good work.

Basic facts relative to The Peace Mission Movement do not appear at all in the analysis you enclosed. The Peace Mission Movement is essentially Christian, based on The Sermon on the Mount. Father's Teaching translates the philosophy of Christianity into the actions of daily living. It is Christianity in action. Nevertheless, all of the books and publications that could ever be written cannot convey the whole truth. To get a true concept a person should *live* the Life of Christ and then come and see.[15]

To return to our own account, during the Sayville period Major Jealous Divine discovered that there were people who wanted only *his* version of himself, *his* history, *his* mission, and addressed himself to them. Conflicts arose with other religious leaders and groups which he sought, unsuccessfully, to avoid. Later he would feel that "every knock is a boost, every attack a victory," for they gave him the chance to present his message. Long before McLuhan Father Divine decided that "the medium is the message" and He was the medium.

He describes himself as at first trying to keep himself, as a person, out of the picture by recommending books that "bear witness of My Teaching and My Views to *some* degree." "I authorized Myself, Personally and Consciously to give out a hundred dollars' worth of books a month." He chose two authors, Robert Collier, who in seven volumes[16] taught a version of "new thought" which promised salvation and prosperity; and Baird T. Spalding, who in three volumes revealed *The Life and Teaching of the Masters of the Far East*.[17]

"I tried to give out the highest Light of the Teaching I could find written in books, that would somewhat convey the Message of Truth, the way I saw it . . . not for it to be an Eternal Expression, or a commercial contribution to humanity, but as a Message at that time to those who had not heard of Me, and had not been quickened and awakened."

The medium was to be the giver, not the books, however, for Father Divine found that his followers would rather listen to him than read them. According to his account:

> Hence, I gave them out for a while, and as soon as I made up My Mind to give out a thousand dollars' worth a month . . . all who came in contact with Me, were touched with the Omnilucence of My Spirit and Mind [and] the the gloom of the human intelligence, the gloom of darkness of the human intellect in this Light of Civilization, was turned into bright noonday. By the Omnilucence of My Spirit, it can no longer be seen nor heard, hence they could not read these books, and neither could I give them out, much less than selling them or being an agent for them.

> When I unfolded Myself in the Spirit of My Presence, and in the Presence of the people, as I Am, they saw no longer need for books and Bibles and Hymn Books. They saw the Spirit of God's Presence was Sufficient, in the fulfillment of the Scriptures: "When He the Spirit of Truth has come, you will need no man to teach you."[18]

Father Divine was truly the medium for the message from this time on. Even his quotations from the Old and New Testaments were inspired, he explained, by his spiritual participation in the events they recorded. In addition to the various publications which recorded and printed his words, sound equipment and tape recorders also substituted for his personal presence. No follower was ever bereft of the sight or sound of Father's words. As Collier and Spalding were no longer read, so all other "religious" writers lost their inspiration for the true follower.

The Reverend Major Jealous Divine knew that he was the medium through which God spoke, and those who agreed with him, who received instruction from him, were his disciples. Their recognition of his extraordinary influence evoked in him the conviction that they preferred *his* message, *his* presence, *his* example to what he often called "the God of Churchianity" or a "God up in the Heavens someplace."

Like Collier, who had advocated a religion of practical success in living a healthy, prosperous life, Father Divine promised as practical results good health for his followers and meeting their needs of "shelter and food and raiment."

In Sayville he apparently accepted as guests all that the home would accommodate. Only a very few have publicly disputed his claim that he charged them nothing.

Many others have risen to testify for "Father," as he was commonly addressed and referred to in meeting.

Without revealing the source of *his* income, but acknowledging that Peninah's hard-earned cash had bought the home, he explained the prosperity of his followers:

> There were some that came out there from Brooklyn with us, some who had lived with us for many, many years. Through My cooperation they had a chance to save their money and be absolutely independent! After a long time some of them had saved up five or six thousand dollars; just domestic workers and common laborers, earning from fifteen to twenty-five dollars a week! They had nothing to spend it for when they were with Me. [They] earned the money and saved it up, and when the time came that I discontinued running the home myself as a Person... they started up to buy homes and open up places such as this one, to do by Me and by others as I had done for them. That is what it is all about![19]

II

Father Divine Recognized as God

At Sayville, Father Divine led a rather quiet life through the twenties. He ran weekly ads in the *Suffolk County News,* offering to supply workers for all sorts of household duties. Gradually more followers came to live with him. By 1924, according to one follower, the group had thirty or forty members. By 1926 it was an integrated group. In 1930 a busload of Holiness Church members of various complexions came to visit from West New York, New Jersey. Some were impressed and converted, as were a number of the "minority group," converted that same year. Eugene Del Mar, who had been in the New Thought movement and a student of Helen Williams, founder of a school of "mental science," endorsed Father Divine. Walter Clemow Lanyon, an English author of mystical and inspirational books, visited Sayville and returned to preach Father Divine's message in England, on the Continent, and in Australia. Christian Science women appeared on the scene and J. Maynard Mathews, a Boston University graduate who gave up his automobile agency to enter the spiritual life as Brother John Lamb, became Father's Executive Secretary.

Thus it was that even the early years of the Movement saw an amalgam of people and beliefs from Holiness, Christian Science, and New Thought, as well as individuals who had already sought salvation or truth outside the major middle-class religious groups. Followers were of all complexions, several ethnic groups, and represented all levels of formal education.

Testimonials given at religious services today often refer to healings which took place many years ago in Sayville. Those who benefited by them always gave Father Divine the credit. The presence of previously segregated persons living, working, and worshipping together helped convince the true believers of Father's charismatic qualities.

Excerpts from testimonies in recent years by followers converted during the

Sayville period, from 1919 to 1934, indicate what experiences, healings, and other effects helped build up charismatic status for Father Divine and his Movement.

Miss Deborah Newmind, who identified herself as having been born into an Orthodox Jewish family, first heard about Father Divine from two "metaphysical lecturers" who had come from Sayville to a Truth Center in Seattle, Washington. They shared with her the following letter from Eugene Del Mar:[1]

EUGENE DEL MAR
ATTORNEY AND COUNSELLOR

51 Macon Street
Sayville, L.I., N.Y.
November 23, 1931

To Whom It May Concern:

My name having been printed in the NEW YORK TIMES as a witness in the proceedings at Sayville, Long Island in connection with "Father Divine," I take this opportunity to give my reasons for being at Sayville, especially as what I found here is a matter of current public interest.

For over thirty years I have been before the public as author, lecturer, teacher and organizer in what has been designated variously as Mental Science, New Thought, Psychology, Spiritual Science, etc.; and I have been in fairly intimate association with hundreds of other teachers who are similarly disposed. My record will be found in most of such general books of reference as Who's Who in America,[2] and from time to time I have been connected with many of the best schools that have functioned or now operate along these lines. I was attracted here to study the life and teachings of one whom I was advised to be a great teacher and healer, besides being gifted with unusual powers.

In the light of this background, I have listened for a full month to the teachings of Father Divine. These are all given at free meals, so that eating and teaching go together. I now recognize in Father Divine one whose love, charity, sympathy and other spiritual attributes are manifested in a transparent purity of life; and to whose wisdom and understanding of spiritual truth I bow my head with reverence. In the words of another epoch: "I find no fault in this man." All that I have seen, felt and ascertained regarding the life and teachings of Father Divine have illumined my understanding beyond anything I have heretofore experienced. His teachings are both extremely simple and deeply profound. They inculcate the practice of the

Christ Life "as recorded in Matthew, Mark, Luke and John," and seemingly
he lives this life in its fullness. He expounds the teachings of Jesus as con-
trasted with those of Paul. This Christ Life he depicts as one of extreme
purity and universal love. He cites the New Testament in support of his
teaching that the results of living this life are peace of mind and health of
body, together with all of the other beautiful possibilities of life. His teaching is that of essential Unity and Oneness: that body, mind and soul are
One; and that when the Christ Life is lived in its fullness, the body is spirit-
ualized so that it partakes of the Spirit of God, and is no longer subject to
Death.

The life so depicted certainly offers a striking contrast to the average
life of humanity, and its practicality may not be understood by the vast majority of mankind. Only in the slightest degree, if any, do the teachings of
Father Divine account for the antagonism toward him; for those who oppose him know little or nothing of his teachings. The opposition is based
on racial color prejudice, intensified by annoyance to neighbors incident to the
sounds of worship, and by alleged loss of village property values. Many of
his enemies are friendly to him personally, for he expresses every admi-
rable quality and is always kind and considerate. In regard to his appearance,
he explains that it is in order that the inherent beauty of the "personal life"
may be detected beneath an unattractive exterior. But his followers find
in him equal beauty of character and countenance.

To many of his followers, Father Divine's unfailing expressions and
activities of love and sympathy, his lofty teachings and purity of life, and
the unusual powers with which he seems to be endowed, impel them to
place him in a category superior to ordinary mortality, and they recognize
in him the expected Messiah. Many address him as "God," "Jesus Christ,"
and in other terms of Divinity. But he states frequently that what he does
all others can do when they think and live as he does and have the same
consciousness.

Some of the familiar biblical quotations are: "I and the Father are
One," "The Father is in me and I am in the Father," and "Know ye not that
ye are the Temple of God?" Some of his own familiar sayings are: "God is
here and there and everywhere," "The Christ in you and the Christ in me
will make you what you ought to be," and "The abundance of the fullness of
the consciousness of God: no space is vacant of the fullness thereof." A few
of the frequent exclamations are "Peace, Father!" "Thank you, Father!"
and "It is wonderful."

Many have been attracted to Father Divine out of curiosity and the fact that he feeds freely and "sumptuously" from, say, 400 to 800 people each day. He accepts no money from anyone, has no bank account, and pays cash for all purchases. His answer to all inquiries as to the source of his financial supply is: "The spirit of the consciousness of the presence of God is the source of all supply and will satisfy every good desire." Among the more intelligent and critical of his guests are those who claim to have actually seen him multiply the food before their very eyes!

Many have come afflicted with various physical disorders and gone away healed, and some of these have returned again and again to testify to the fact. But Father Divine constantly advises that the permanence of healing is dependent upon the continued purity of life. He does not claim that personally he heals anyone, or that it is necessary to contact him personally for that purpose. He states that it is "your faith" that heals you, and that you can contact him mentally and spiritually at any distance with the same result. Many testify that they have called upon his name from a distance and have been healed—sometimes instantaneously!

Highly educated scholars have been here who have accorded to Father Divine unique and exceptional attributes; but no one has as yet solved the mystery underlying his personality, wisdom, supply and power. Now that the press and radio have spread the news of his activities near and far, Father Divine has become a world figure, whose presence and significance can no longer be ignored. It seems to be the mission and hidden purpose of all persecutions to bring into the light of public interest that which otherwise might remain in the twilight of comparative indifference.

[Signed] Eugene Del Mar

Having heard this letter, Miss Newmind went from Seattle to Oakland, California, where, she says:

I found one follower and then many others—one testified of her instantaneous healing of cancer in the last stages, after all the doctors had given her up when her mother wrote a letter.... This daughter and this mother testified again and again that this girl was dying in the very last stages of cancer; that the doctors refused to come to the house any more. When her mother wrote a letter to Sayville to Father Divine, she was instantaneously and miraculously healed![3]

Miss Newmind, who became a follower in the 1930s, testified many years later to further healings of "incurable" illnesses, to English followers who slept through the blitz "like children," and even young followers "at the battlefront" who came through without a scratch.

Other believers who remained convinced for many years recollected "miracles" in the early days at a reunion banquet at Sayville in March 1961.

Miss Queen Esther, who had come to see Father Divine there about 1940, spoke of herself when she said: "Father, you healed her eyes that night, because she could not see her own name unless it was engraved in big letters. You healed her eyes and her stomach and that whole body."[4]

Miss St. Theresa told of her leap back to health:

> You healed me and I didn't even know you healed me but I was so well and healthy that I just went on to work and started to work! Before that I was in and out of the hospitals, and the doctors didn't have any help for me.

Although Father Divine did not know her personally at the time, nor even where she lived, she described the "visitation" that she believed happened:

> Father, you came in there in a little blue suit and a black tie and called me by that name I had. And, Father, when I looked and saw you, I almost died! Father, I was so frightened! But you said, you held up your hand like this, Father. And Father, the light and the rays went out from your hand so beautiful and you said, "I am the light of the world and I came to take away the sins of the world!" And Father, all that fear fell off me and I fell back to sleep, and I don't know when you left there.

The next day she was so happy she danced and "went to tell the people that God is Here, Father Divine is God Almighty."[5]

Thousands of such witnesses of healing and "visitation" could be heard during the services of the various Peace Mission Churches, and culled from the *Spoken Word*, 1933–1937, the *World Herald*, 1935–1937, and the *New Day*, 1938 to the present. New testimony is still brought out at any of the church services today (1978).

In addition to the healings and "visitations" credited to Father Divine another source of his charisma was the growing conviction that Father Divine could make a "sinner" become self-respecting and self-supporting. Little David's testimony is a typical sample:

> I was a bootlegger, I lived a very wicked life. . . . I liked to run around and liked to go places. . . . I said as long as anybody has a dollar and they drank whiskey I was going to have money. . . . I started a joint . . . a fight started . . . It was broken up. You, Father, knocked every prop out from under me,

causing me to be hungry. . . . I wondered how I would ever get back on my feet again. . . . I hung around bus places and picked up cigarette butts. . . . I went to the different agencies . . . the panic was on . . . they said, "There is not anything we can do for you." . . . I didn't want to get on the breadline, but I did . . . then the bread was all mouldy . . . then I heard about Sayville. . . . I got a job at the Public Service.[6]

Little David, who has long been a follower, also attributes his good health to Father Divine: "When I came to you I was little and skinny. A little thirty-two belt used to lap around me, Father, and you put flesh on the bones and healed the body and took me out of TB when I was so poor and frail."[7]

The following account from the *New Day*[8] of an interview with Father Divine is an example of how he dealt with the problem of illness. He sometimes added that if the individual did not have enough faith in God for the condition to improve in three days, a physician should be consulted.

FATHER DIVINE

INTERVIEW

GRANTED TO MRS. R.

SEEKING HEALING

In Father's Office
Brigantine Hotel
Brigantine, N.J.

Saturday, September 26th, 1942 A.D.F.D.

As with all who come seeking the blessings of life and health and peace, FATHER so lovingly on this occasion gave to this individual the key to happiness and health which she was diligently seeking.

A beautiful parable was given by FATHER of a mother's understanding care for her child, to bring out the mystery of our Mother-God's skill in creating a substantial and unshaken faith in God, in His children of Righteousness.

For the enlightenment of all, these words are printed for your salvation. Read and live!

[The foregoing statements are those of the transcriber, and the interview follows:]

Secretary: Father, this is Mrs. R., Mrs. O. R.

FATHER: PEACE, Mrs. R.; take a seat.

Mrs. R: FATHER, this is a moment of my life that I have prayed for. I wanted to see You and ask You, will You please better my condition. It is
so hard for me to speak. It's my throat, FATHER.

FATHER: You have said you have . . .

Mrs. R: Bronchitis. But I know You know. Yes, and I want You to please
give me health and strength to make conditions better—bind my
family together, please, Sir.

FATHER: I see. Well, it is not anything I do as a person to reach one's condition, but as you make your mental and Spiritual contact through
harmonization and through sympatheticness with this Truth exemplified among you, your desires, which are your prayers, will be heard
and answered. Hence, you can be healthy, matters not what may be
your ailment.

Mrs. R: Thank you, FATHER.

FATHER: It depends altogether on your faith. Some are healed gradually;
but it is according to the development of your faith.

Mrs. R: Father, I feel so much better since I have been in the hotel here.

FATHER: Sure! Well, it is as I explained last evening in part. It is the atmosphere that has been created by the consciousness of GOD's Presence. It is not because this is some way or some place different from
other places as far as Spirituality or divine ecstasy is concerned. We
have it by the consciousness of GOD's Presence, which creates an atmosphere which is the Spirit of the Consciousness of GOD'S PRES-
ENCE that automatically adjusts matters satisfactorily. When you are
conscious of undesirable representatives of life and of death, why
then, you create such a condition resulting from your consciousness
concerning such a situation and such persons. Therefore you bring
into your own life and into your own experience that which results
from such a state of consciousness.

In being in this hotel, you will contact the unfoldment of the Spirit of
MY Presence through the consciousness of those who are conscious of

MY Presence and who recognize MY Presence as being supernatural and not natural.

Mrs. R: Yes.

FATHER: By this it causes the Spirit of the supernatural to be in evidence in your experience, which is in reality a healing balm to your soul. It does not mean that I would exercise any physical activity to reach one's condition, and I do not use material remedies. I do not use or make physical efforts to reach one's mind, nor with material methods, but as one makes the mental and Spiritual contact, the spirit of GOD'S Presence actually creates a harmonious condition.

The same as a mother soothes the child's feeling, both in mind and body. The mother can take up a little child and kiss it if it falls down and hurts itself and tell the child it is all right.

Mrs. R: So true!

FATHER: That is the significance of metaphysical truth. Even the metaphysicians teach such as affirmation being a positive assertion that will bring out the desirable results, and some who are not metaphysicians and may not be considered as metaphysically inclined, but the mother of almost every child will tell the little child that. They use psychology; they use the method of the metaphysicians by assertion and by making an affirmation in an assertion that results in the condition of the child, and the child is usually healed because he believes what his mother says. And so it is with the children of GOD when as a little child, you see, you have been converted and have become fit meat for the Master's use and . . .

Mrs. R: Yes, LORD.

FATHER: . . . and a fit subject for the Kingdom, it is that person who has actually been converted and becomes as a little child. Hence, whatsoever the Spirit of the consciousness of GOD'S Presence reveals to them or tells them, they believe it, you see. It may not come as a dream or a vision, but it might come as an individual revelation that would be given individually. You get a thought within, you are in GOD'S Presence and He has said,

"It is well with your soul," and such a . . .

Mrs. R: Thank GOD!

FATHER: . . . condition of being materializes. Physically you are made well because of your faith you have in Him Who has said it.

Mrs. R: Thank you, FATHER.

FATHER: So it is a wonderful thought. Now if you take these thoughts to consideration, as you say you have felt much better and have improved so much since you have been here; just keep ME in consciouness harmoniously and MY spirit and MY presence will continue to work just as effectively when you return to your home. But live in harmony and in keeping with MY Teaching and bring your body into subjection to the life and the teaching of JESUS as recorded in the four Gospels, your simplest prayer is heard and answered; and prayer is the heart's sincere desire unuttered and unexpressed.

Mrs. R: Oh, so true!

FATHER: One writer said:

"We know not what we should pray for as we ought."

I know your human intelligence is inadequate to know how to make the petition to GOD and pray as you ought, but

"The Spirit," the writer said, it "maketh intercession
in groanings which cannot be uttered."

Mrs. R: Oh, glory!

FATHER: So you may rest assured, according to your faith, self-denial and consecration, so be it unto you. Your prayers are heard and answered and you may go on your way rejoicing and do not allow such conditions to result again, for such conditions come through doubts and fears and through negative and conflicting thinking or thoughts.

Mrs. R: Yes, FATHER, there seems to be so much trouble.

FATHER: Yes, thinking of trouble and believing in trouble. To the reverse, you believe in GOD and believe in happiness, PEACE and joy—the extreme reverse to that of trouble, and you will find everything will be all right.

Mrs. R: Thank you, FATHER, and may I meet you again. Please don't forget me.

FATHER: Keep the faith and live the life and everything will be all right. Peace!

Mrs. R: Peace, FATHER!

Healing alone could not account for Father Divine's charisma; healing was not unknown in minority group churches, and several of his followers were Christian Science practitioners when they joined his Movement.[9] At least as supernatural, in his followers' eyes, was his ability to contend with great social forces and institutions. His success in this area seemed phenomenal and validated his charisma for many.

That Father Divine could, in the eyes of his followers, defeat the government when it pleased him to spurn its aid seemed miraculous. By having his followers refuse unemployment insurance, workmen's compensation, social security, and public assistance he proved to them that they could prosper, even in depression. If a follower did not prosper it was not God's fault nor the government's, but lack of faith in Father Divine. Blame could also be shifted to "the other fellow" (the Movement's euphemism for the devil) or to racial discrimination. As in the Protestant ethic, according to Weber's theory, predestination to salvation or damnation was verified by hard work and success in this world.

According to Weber, for the Calvinist:

> The world exists to serve the glorification of God and for that purpose alone. The elected Christian is in the world only to increase the Glory of God by fulfilling His commandments to the best of his ability. But God requires social achievement of the Christian because He wills that a social life shall be organized according to His commandments, in accordance with that purpose. The social activity of the Christian in the world is solely activity *in majorem gloriam Dei*. This character is hence shared by labour in a calling which serves the mundane life of the community.... Brotherly love, since it may only be practiced for the glory of God and not in the service of the flesh, is expressed in the fulfillment of the daily tasks given by the *lex naturae*; and in the process this fulfillment assumes a peculiarly objective and impersonal character, that of service in the interest of the rational organization of our social environment.[10]

Father Divine moved God and Heaven to this earth and turned the idea of predestination for an other-worldly heaven into the idea of predestination for a this-worldly heaven. But the emphasis on mundane employment "in the interest of the rational organization of our social environment," remained.

Followers who did not work to support themselves and the Movement were strongly encouraged to do so. There is indeed "an objective and impersonal" character to the way in which the followers regard those who will not pull their weight in the organization.

The first event in which Father Divine's intercession demonstrated that he had power greater than the government's was the death of Supreme Court Justice Lewis J. Smith.

By 1931, Father Divine's fame had spread to Harlem and busloads of worshippers and sightseers were coming out to Sayville on weekends. Neighbors' objections to the religious services and traffic congestion culminated in a police raid on Sunday, November 15, 1931. Eighty attenders who were arrested—fifteen of them of the American majority group—were charged with "disturbing the peace." Fifty-five pleaded guilty and paid a five-dollar fine. Father Divine and twenty-five others pleaded not guilty and were brought to trial.

Father Divine told the court that this was racial discrimination and violated his constitutional rights. Afro-American papers and the press services picked up the case. Correspondence sprang up with sympathizers all over the country, some primarily interested in the discrimination issue, others wanting to hear more about the religion. Eugene Del Mar's letter was inspired by the *New York Times* accounts on November 17, 21, and 22, 1931.[11] The Long Island trial made Father Divine a national figure in the eyes of his followers, and he attracted national publicity from then on.

A Harlem lawyer, James C. Thomas, former U.S. Assistant District Attorney, offered his services for the trial in the interest of challenging racial discrimination, and Arthur Madison, another Harlem lawyer, although not a follower, testified on Father Divine's behalf. From then on lawyers figured prominently in his activities.

The Bill of Particulars against Father stated:

> Defendant claimed to be the Messiah returned to earth; conducted so-called religious services, at which services colored and white people did congregate in large numbers; and did then and there exhort people in loud tones of voice and did then and there encourage, aid and assist those present in shouting and singing in loud tones, annoying neighbors in the vicinity of the defendant's place.

And did then and there permit and encourage large numbers of people on foot and in autos to gather around the place; and did encourage said singing, shouting, exhorting and stamping to continue past midnight, keeping them awake at all hours of the night and morning.

The judge's attitude and tone at the trial made the racial issue very evident. When several white followers testified that they knew Father Divine was God, and John Lamb said that Father's finances were arranged by the Universal Mind Substance, the judge questioned the sanity of Father Divine's followers. But the court could find no evidence that any of them had been committed to a mental hospital.

The judge asked for the maximum sentence, including in his charge to the jury the still unproved accusation: "His name is not Divine . . . he is not an ordained minister . . . he is not married to the woman he calls his wife . . . he has another woman as his wife and has children living . . . he takes his followers' wages and has used them for his own purpose . . . he has failed to cooperate."[12]

On May 25, 1932, the jury found him guilty but advocated leniency since he had never been convicted of crime and planned as soon as possible to leave the county. On Saturday, June 5, Judge Smith sentenced him to one year in the county jail and fined him $500, the maximum penalty under the law.

Two days later Judge Smith, an apparently healthy man, died of a heart attack. Father Divine's followers immediately interpreted this as an act of retribution brought about by Father's wrath. It was a turning point in his career.

Ever since that day—June 7, 1932—Father Divine and his followers have publicized incidents of death and suffering striking down persons who did not "harmonize" with Father Divine. The *New Day* printed many such references, a few of which will illustrate their nature:

> If I do not have free access in any part of this country and especially where they oppose me, ambulances and doctors and the Red Cross will go to see them.[13]

In a telephone conversation with a reporter in connection with the refusal of Yonkers, New York, officials to give him a license to parade, Father Divine said:

> You see, when prejudice tries to bar the peaceful access and the peaceful assemblage of any peaceful people, naturally the cosmic forces of nature go forth destructively and act as they would desire to act towards those to whom they are prejudiced. . . .My home will not be disturbed, even as it was not disturbed the other week. All the telephone communication was

cut off in that community and also in New Rochelle, and My Home was in perfect contact with the outside world. So that thought you had just as well to know—those who are malicious to that degree, or prejudiced, they might know if they try to bar Me, I will bar them through the cosmic forces of nature or in some other way they may not think.[14]

In a letter to the president of an international airlines organization, Father Divine asserted not only that airplane accidents were caused by ignoring his message and indulging in discrimination, but that every other calamity was rooted in the same cause. The Second World War could have been avoided "had they taken cognizance of MY message." The "very ground itself is cursed" when "men seek to segregate themselves and place restrictions on deeds and papers." "Where prejudice, division, bigotry and strife exist, disaster also exists or follows. The Texas City fire, the floods in the Middle West and the many airplane crashes, train wrecks, and automobile wrecks attest the fact."[15]

Many followers were convinced of Father Divine's powers by the death of Judge Smith. Father Divine was evidently greater than the government. If someone in government practiced discrimination, it seemed that retribution would occur, and Father Divine would be still more powerful.

An Appellate Court reversal of Judge Smith's trial conviction was a triumphant anticlimax. A new trial was ordered because "prejudice was excited in the jurors by the comments, rulings and questions by the court." The case was never retried, and its significance was never forgotten by the followers: Only God could punish the judge and overcome the law.

Father Divine was free again, although he had spent thirty-three days in jail.

From this point on the followers proclaimed the divinity of their leader at meetings, at parades, at various legal proceedings in which the Movement became involved, and in their weekly newspaper. Accused of being evasive in court, Father Divine did not hesitate to declare himself God before his own followers and visitors, nor did he avoid having his own remarks printed for all to read.

The followers gained a sense of unity and continuous participation in the activities of "God" through the Movement's weekly "newspapers" which published all Father Divine's public utterances. They treated these utterances as God's commands for their daily lives and considered nothing too trivial for the Father to control. As Wilson observes:

Sectarians often display a hugh regard for charismatic authority whether this be offered as an incarnation of God in man, as a special anointing by

God as a prophet, or merely as a marked natural ability, special wisdom, knowledge, lucidity or unction. The leader is responsible, at least initially and in part, for the precepts and examples which his votaries accept, and for the primary articulation of values to which they subscribe: his self-interpretation conditions their behavior and beliefs.[16]

Since the charismatic leader's self-interpretation is so central to the principles of the Peace Mission Church, we shall devote the next chapter largely to quotations from Father Divine, projecting the image of himself which he had verbalized for thirty years.

III

Father
Divine
Is
God

"Read my messages with an open heart and mind and you will learn of ME, and receive Truths, such as man has never given. You are not dealing with man, but with GOD."[1]

The Movement's publications have never ceased to assert that Father Divine is God. They still expound in Father Divine's words on the "ideal culture" which God (Father Divine) expects everyone to practice. The letter containing the quotation above offers Father Divine's basic ideology for the Peace Mission Movement.[2] Presumably, it represents what the leadership of the Movement still believes to be the nature and mission of Father Divine and the spiritual basis for the religious "community" calling itself the International Peace Mission Movement: "You will find MY International Peace Mission Movement . . . is the Christian Movement (for it is founded upon Christ's Sermon on the Mount) is not operated according to any denominational church, neither is it patterned after any material plan of man."[3]

By establishing his Movement as *the* Christian movement, not an ordinary church, Father Divine conveyed the idea that the Sermon on the Mount was *his* sermon, since he was, and continued to be, Christ. His Movement was of God, since he was God, whereas all other religious groups were patterned by man.

Concerning the Peace Mission Movement, he said:

> Daniel of the Scripture spoke of it, and it is fulfilled this day in your midst:
>
> "And in the days of these kings, shall the God of heaven set up a kingdom, which shall never be destroyed: and the kingdom shall not be left to other people, but it shall break in pieces and consume all these kingdoms, and it shall stand forever." (Daniel 2:44)

MY Kingdom is not being established as man would think it would, for as Jesus conveyed:

"The kingdom of God cometh not with observation: Neither shall they say, Lo here! or lo there! for behold, the kingdom of God is within you." (St. Luke 17:20–21)[4]

If it is read and understood in terms of the Movement's "sacred literature," this statement presents the doctrine that the Movement is the Kingdom predicted in the Bible and established by God (who is also Father Divine); it is indestructible and will eventually triumph over all other "kingdoms"; it has no particular location in space but is "found within you."

In one sense, the Kingdom is God working within the hearts and minds of men; but it "tangibilates" (to use an original word of Father's) itself in a set of folkways, mores, values, ideologies, and attitudes, supreme among which is the worship of Father Divine as God. As the founder put it in his own language:[5]

I have come in this Fatherhood Dispensation fulfilling the Scripture from A to Z; from Genesis to Revelation, moving in all fields of life, for indeed GOD deals in the affairs of men.

I do not work like man. I work on the Inside, for I work in the hearts and minds of the children of men; thus bringing about the true concepts of the Christ mind and cause the people to live according to their new birth of freedom, such as Jesus said to Nicodemus: "Ye must be born again."

Millions all over the world who follow ME, no longer live in dishonesty, sin, vice and crime; nor do they indulge in the carnal pleasures of men and women, but they live virtuous and pure in *mind* and *body* just as Mary lived before Jesus was born, and as Jesus Christ lived, the way-shower for all mankind, for He declared:

"I am the way, the truth, and the life: no man cometh unto the Father but by me." (St. John 14:6).

MY presence within them directs them in the positive way to go.

All the various Connections—the Churches and Extensions of MY International Peace Mission Movement are established by individuals, or groups of individuals who cooperate together and dedicate their purchases to the Cause. MY SPIRIT does the work; that is, I work by the inspiration of the Spirit, directing all by the Omniscience of MY Presence.

Thus, without establishing anything I heal the sick and raise the dead. . . . I eradicate all the vices of men by injecting the Holiness of MY Mind and Spirit in them, making them honest, competent, virtuous and true from every angle expressible.[6]

As if anticipating criticism of pie-in-the-sky religion, God gives very down-to-earth suggestions, such as advice to associate only with those who do not get in trouble, to stay away from temptation. One letter signed "Rev. M. J. Divine" demonstrates how "commonsense" suggestions for social acceptance were combined by this Movement with mystical ideas and the psychology of positive thinking.

Replying to a correspondent who wrote that he knew the truth, but nevertheless had been charged with committing a crime, Father Divine warned of the harm that "socialization" with the wrong associates could do to a human being:

It is possible . . . for a person to be found in the company of gamblers, drunkards, wine-bibbers, prostitutes, narcotics users and the like and be innocent as you imply Christ was found in such company and adjudged guilty, although HE was innocent. Nevertheless, I declare it would take nothing less than the CHRIST unadulterated to be found in such company and be uncontaminated by such a company. Hence, if you were found in such company and you are not the CHRIST unadulterated, then no doubt the court found justification for condemning you, even though you say you are innocent; for usually a man is known by the company he keeps.

It reminds ME of a little story, which you may have heard or read as I have told it often:

A crane or stork was keeping company with the crows and the farmer caught the stork and he said to the farmer, "I do not eat corn—I have not been eating your corn!" The farmer said "Yes, but you were in the crowd! You are one of the gang!"

So the thought goes, "A man is known by the company he keeps!" Evil communications corrupt good morals. Ill qualities are catching as well as disease.[7]

He wound up with positive advice to associate only with responsible people of good reputation, whose good traits might then be passed on to him:

Hence, it behooves you if you desire to be truthful, if you desire to be successful, if you desire to be prosperous, if you desire to be any of these desirable qualities all humanity is seeking, qualify yourself in the Unity of Spirit, of Mind, of Aim and of Purpose with those who are the expressors of them.[8]

Launching into ideology, with references to the exemplary spirit of God, he issued, in the following letter, admonitions and instructions which his followers had been absorbing for thirty years or more:

> As I often say, the very LIFE OF GOD, the SPIRIT OF GOD, the MIND OF GOD, and all of GOD'S Characteristics are IMPERSONAL and just as expressive for the IMPERFECT as they are for the PERFECT, if the IMPERFECT qualify themselves to express them!

> Then I say permit MY characteristics as exemplified, the qualities of GOD as demonstrated, to be manifested in you by harmonizing with the GREAT PRINCIPLES as exemplified among you. Thus, by living accordingly even though you may be found in the world, you will not be of the world.[9]

Again, a typical letter indicates Father Divine's conviction that he is God, establishing the Kingdom of God and heaven here on earth. He identifies this Kingdom with a Family (the "one Family of God"), brotherhood, racial equality, liberty, and justice. A quotation from the Bible links this statement with earlier ones when he spoke through or as Christ. Although these are later examples, the practice of identifying himself and his utterances with the pronouncements of sacred personages in the Old and New Testament was consistent throughout his recorded career.

As this letter progresses, the speaker "HE" (Christ) becomes the speaker (I Father Divine):

> The LORD hath prepared his throne in the heavens; and his kingdom ruleth over all. [Divine is referring to some statement he attributes to David and Jesus.]

> In referring to this harmony above the mortal turmoil of the earth, Christ prayed:

> "Thy kingdom come. Thy will be done in earth as in Heaven." (Matt. 6:10)

> In effect He was teaching mankind to visualize that state of harmony that is above what you have called "creed-prattle, shrieking intolerance, racial superiority claims and the lack of brotherhood" so that the Liberty, Justice and Equality of the One Family of GOD might be established on earth or in earth.

In Woodmont [the most magnificent of the Movement's properties] you have beheld what the prophets, the sages and the seers have envisioned. In this reality of Democracy, you have enjoyed a foretaste of what it shall be from shore to shore and from land to land when I have finished the work of MY mission.

Then I say, if each and everyone will live by the Principles of Righteousness, Justice and Truth which produce PEACE, by the SPIRIT of MY PRESENCE I shall eventually bring all mankind into the Unity of the Spirit, of Mind, of Aim and of Purpose, if they live. Those who refuse to come together as "one man at Jerusalem" shall not have access on the earth. By MY PRESENCE and the STANDARD I AM LIFTING I AM judging the world and producing PEACE on EARTH to all men of good will.

Thus, I appreciate your gratitude for MY Presence for I delight in blessing mankind, especially those who are not afraid to speak the Truth and stand for that which they know to be Just and Right.[10]

Photographs as well as words have been used extensively in both the sacred literature of the Movement and in the secular press to convey the presence of God. For a number of years the front page of the *New Day,* from its first issue in 1937, carried a photograph of Father Divine every week. It was always a dignified portrait, even on the July 14, 1938, cover which showed him posing with a horse at an Ulster County, New York, farm which some followers then owned.

In the portraits which appeared over the years in most newspapers and newsmagazines Father Divine was usually dressed in a conservative black or blue suit and white shirt. For a parade, in the country, or in summertime, he might have worn a light colored suit or a conservative tweed, but never "sporty" clothes or bizarre attire. In playing down his physical appearance, Father Divine maintained:

> I could do many things to make MYSELF Personally appear to be more than what I really AM, so far as man would take ME to be. I do not wear garbs and robes and a whole lot of foolishness, to appear to men as though I AM GOD and still be a man. I would rather appear, so far as physical appearance is concerned, the same as any other man and still be GOD, than to be beguiled firstly with the "beguilation" of Eve MYSELF, to try to make someone else think I AM GOD by My Physical Appearance . . . trying to make myself appear in some way that I AM not."

This image was compatible with the kind of value system which this Movement evolved—a modification of the "Protestant Ethic," as defined by Weber.[12]

Even at religious services, held nightly in the halls of the various churches and missions scattered throughout Philadelphia, Harlem, Brooklyn, Newark, and Connecticut, Father Divine never appeared in clerical clothing. Instead he would wear a neatly pressed "business suit," decorated only with a lapel pin and sometimes a few pens or pencils in the breast pocket. Robes and elaborate garb he considered fit only for pastors, preachers, ministers, and such self-styled emissaries of God as Daddy Grace[13] for whom Father Divine had little respect. God does not need them. As a "man" Father Divine did not seek to impress anyone: ("I could try to make myself look pretty, too, but I forbid!"). As a God:

> I AM what I AM; and you see ME as I AM, as I have heard some say, "I see YOU as YOU is." It matters not what they say, I understand them. They may make grammatical errors, for I make them with them for a purpose, that they might understand ME; that I might be with them in their grammatical errors, and erroneousness; that I might lift them and they might lift ME. Aren't you glad?

> I speak! I act! I stand! I go! I come! I fill all space and I AM absent from none. If HE were limited to perfection as man classes perfection why HE would not be OMNIPOTENT, for there is some power in imperfection. There is some power and wisdom and knowledge in ignorance.

> Oh, it is a privilege to observe the mystery! There is where the universe at large, the great men have missed it, by failing to get it. I thank you.[14]

The body's Godhood speaks for itself in literally millions of words, even ungrammatical ones, contradictory ones, and newly invented ones. If you see the mystery it is a privilege, for even great men have missed it! With this kind of logic Father Divine did not have to dress like other preachers. He merely spoke and acted like God, and taught his followers that God has a right to be himself. He assured the ungrammatical, the ignorant, the imperfect that by identifying themselves with God they were being wiser than "the great men."

The earliest written record of Father Divine's theology and philosophy appeared as a statement in the New Day, September 23, 1961, datelined Sayville Banquet Table 1931.

The essence of this message, couched in the language of occult literature and New Thought, was that one should give up one's body to God, strongly implied to be Father Divine. "I don't care," he said, "if I have a body or not if I, as the Great Universal Mind Substance, choose to continue to subjugate the Body to 'I,' the True Infinite Spirit and Universal Mind Substance, it is all right." The theme pervading the rest of the sermon was: "Give up your body for the Spirit's sake and recognize the Spirit and the Life as supreme; and when you do that you are seeking the Kingdom of Heaven; you are looking to the Heavenly state of consciousness and not to the material or mortal state—and shall then all of those things that are material . . . be added unto you."

This one value of the Movement was reiterated thousands of times in different words: Give your body and mind to God, think positively and you will have both material and spiritual success here on earth.

But the most important value was that Father Divine alone could make it possible to know who and what God was and how to meet each contingency of life. With or without a Body, Father Divine was God and the door to unity with God. "I have set before you an open example and also an open door and those of you that are spirit of MY spirit and mind of MY Mind . . . you are the spiritual sons of GOD."

A long quotation from Father Divine—a summary statement of a typical message delivered in 1938—will do much to convey the ethos in which the followers lived:

> Then I say, the last enemy to be conquered is DEATH! You must rise to this place in consciousness where you will be able to conquer death, even as JESUS did, the first born among many brethren, conquering capital punishment in His day. The same Spirit is speaking today! There is no place so high, there is no place so low, that GOD HIMSELF, through His condescension, cannot go there and bring Himself out VICTORIOUSLY a CONQUEROR!
>
> If He cannot bring Himself from "the other place" as He did before[15] why then the time has come He should go! Aren't you glad! GOD is VICTORIOUS over everything, over every mortal version, over every opposition, over every difficulty, over every trial, over every tribulation; and if GOD cannot overcome them all, then let Him GO! I am not talking about letting Him go to a pleasant place, but let Him go to "the other place"! He will make HEAVEN out of "the other place"! That is GOD'S BUSINESS!
>
> GOD is the MASTER of all! Aren't you glad! I say, aren't you glad. If GOD has not POWER over "the other place," then let him GO THERE and STAY there! . . . and let all of His FOLLOWERS go with HIM! Aren't you glad! (Great demonstrations of vibrational emotions greeted these dynamic words of the Lord.)
>
> GOD is the MASTER OF OMNIPOTENCY! GOD is the MASTER of the INFINITENESS of all things; therefore if He cannot control them and

still have VICTORY, then let them overcome Him. THERE IS NO QUES-
TION IN THIS MATTER WITH ME! Matters not what may be said, and
matters not what may be done, GOD in His Own OMNISCIENCE AND
OMNIPOTENCE has all DOMINANCE, and none can hinder HIM!

Jot these words down in your memory, in your notebooks and in your vo-
cabularies and remember them now, once and forever; for GOD is OMNI-
POTENT, OMNISCIENT, and OMNIPRESENT, and the MASTER OF
OMNIPOTENCY and the CONTROLLER of all humanity's destiny, and
NONE can hinder! Aren't you glad!

Truly might one have said:

> "He came treading the winepress all alone and
> of the people there was none to help."

If anything could overcome HIM, even death, He had a right to be overcome! Now aren't you glad!

GOD is the MASTER OF OMNIPOTENCY! GOD is the CONTROLLER
of your DESTINY, and NONE can hinder ME, now henceforth and forever, with or without a BODY! . . . the SAME today, yesterday and forever!
. . . and TELL them all, I said it! I thank you.[16]

IV

God
in
One
Person:
Challenge
and
Answer

Since Father Divine appeared on the scene as a minister, he held public meetings and was questioned about religion. He was repeatedly called upon to define the relationships between God and man. As early as the 1930s his followers accepted him as God.[1] The following account in the *New Day*[2] in 1938 of an exchange that took place at the Banquet Table illustrates his typical way of defining the relationship between himself, God, and man. It appeared under a headline also quoting Father Divine: "I will cause the insignificant and under-privileged to express perfection and produce superiority if they will cooperate with me." After he had preached a sermon on this theme, a visitor responded to his invitation to speak. Father Divine said, as usual at all services:

> We have a good many visiting friends this afternoon, no doubt; if there are any person or persons who would like to have a word to say, as I often say, you are welcome to speak and move volitionally, if you wish to. But if, according to the custom of the children of men, if you are speakers, religious speakers, ministers of the Gospel, political speakers, or any other speaker, and you desire to have a word to say, if you are accustomed to being called upon, and being introduced, we will gladly introduce you if you desire to be introduced. Give us your name and address, if necessary. I thank you.[3]

> [The editor notes:][4] (A woman who had come into the services early, with a Bible under her arm, and who has been coming to the Sunday afternoon meetings apparently with a dissentious spirit for some few weeks, took advantage of the invitation, and in the same hostile way in which she had made previous approaches, she questioned:)

> "FATHER DIVINE, DO YOU say YOU are GOD? Excuse me, but I can-

not understand." (Turning to the Followers she remarked), "Why do you call HIM GOD? Because GOD said, "I AM GOD, and Jesus My Son came to call you back to God."

[The editor notes:] (By the confused state of the individual, she could hardly hear what FATHER is explaining to her, for she asked a question, she gave her own answer, and talked away at a rapid pace, cutting in constantly as FATHER sought to give her light. FATHER softly answering said:)

"If you are sincere you will understand."

The Individual: I have to ask one more question. Excuse me, I have to ask again, "Does FATHER DIVINE say I AM GOD." Pardon me, FATHER DIVINE, do you say, "I AM GOD?"

FATHER: This is broken English. I will tell you in your hearts, if you DENY yourself and do what Jesus Christ says do. Do you understand that?

The Individual: I don't understand.

FATHER: I say, if you DENY yourself and if you follow Jesus Christ, I will tell you just exactly Who I AM.

The Individual: I am a Follower of Jesus Christ. Jesus Christ is my Redeemer, but Jesus said, "I will come back to the earth." I cannot understand how YOU are GOD!

FATHER: Did Jesus not say in the Gospel, "My FATHER and I will come and make our abode with you"?

The Individual: Yes, but if YOU are GOD, then what is Jesus?

FATHER: I AM all of them. Jesus said, "My Father and I are One," and the Holy Spirit all combined.

The Individual: But listen, Sir! If YOU are the ALMIGHTY, the poor people in Germany can't see YOU! Where is their happiness?

FATHER: GOD IS OMNIPRESENT. GOD IS OMNIPRESENT, but if you take it the way you do take it, and the way millions of others of your type of Religion take it, Jesus would be in Heaven, is that right? Is HE not? And GOD is in Heaven, is HE not? And where is Heaven? It is above the sky, according to your version.

The Individual: Heaven is very large. We do not know the space nor way.

FATHER: It is above all of the suns, the moon and the stars, according to your version.

The Individual: Our understanding is, GOD has provided a place for us: as soon as we die, we get lifted up to Heaven.

FATHER: It is distinctly understood that according to the "Orthodox" Religion and according to the Christian Religion, the majority of them observe GOD to be in Heaven. Of course, we know it is only superstition from that angle of expression, the way they imagine; but if you take it from that angle of expression if GOD is in Heaven above all of the stars, the moon, and all of the other planets, why, it would have taken GOD ten thousand years, in the Name of Jesus to go to some of the far distant stars. It has been shown conclusively by modern science, that there is a star that fills the Solar System, according to one of the recent statements given out a few weeks ago.... There is a star discovered that fills or could fill all of the whole Solar System, it is so great in size. Now to say that CHRIST is above all of the stars,—why, at light-rate speed, or at the speed of light-rate, I might say, it would take ten thousand years for the light-rate speed to go to some of the far-distant stars, and taking ten thousand years to go there, still there are further distant stars far beyond the observation of those who have sought to find out even from an astronomical point of view.... We find that Jesus could not have been to those stars for it has only been one thousand nine hundred and thirty-eight years since Jesus and around less than six thousand years since the beginning of the Creation; so it is plain to see that according to your version, you are mistaken. You are only going by the theories and doctrines of men. You are not going by facts. You are only going by the superstitious ideas and opinions of them; those who have lived in that imaginary concept concerning Spiritual things. Then I say, when you lift your mind from the mortal version of things and allow CHRIST to come in and reign, the Spirit of My PRESENCE will reveal the mystery, for the Kingdom of GOD is right here with you.

The Individual: Do I understand that YOU have born Jesus Christ? If YOU are the FATHER of Jesus Christ, GOD the FATHER, GOD the Son and GOD the Holy Spirit?

FATHER: If you desire to know, it is better revealed than told. Your finite human mind, although intelligent, cannot fathom out the mysteries of GOD. These things must be revealed. Humanity with all of its civilization and with all of the vocabularies of civilization, is not a percent of a fraction of a grain of a percent of a fraction of a grain of GOD'S OMNISCIENCE.

The Individual: Pardon me, Sir. Just a moment, Sir! I respect YOU as a high-class Preacher, as a Follower of Jesus Christ, who follows in His Footsteps. As much as I know of these people who were gangsters and criminals like I was before I met Jesus and before I was born again, but I cannot, I *cannot* believe YOU are GOD.

FATHER: That is up to you. We are not asking you to believe I AM GOD.

The Individual: I would believe if I could believe, but I cannot believe, Sir.

FATHER: We are not asking you to believe. It is immaterial to Me whether you do or not. It is immaterial to ME, I say, whether you do or not. If you wish to testify you are welcome to testify, but trying to correct anyone here, we're not bothering about anyone correcting or making corrections. If you wish to testify, as I say, you are welcome to testify, and your version is as much right to you as ours is to us; therefore, we are not bothering whether you believe I AM or not, only if you ask the questions, and say you cannot understand and desire to understand, I say I will cause you to understand, if you are sincere. GOD in His Own OMNISCIENCE can reach all men and all mankind.

Now in reference to Jesus being in Heaven, according to the Christian version, if GOD is up there, how is it GOD can take care of you and everybody else?

The Individual: Well you see—

FATHER: Well, that is just the way it is with ME. Now I AM in Germany. I Am in Germany now, and I AM elsewhere by the Spirit and by the Mind just like you surmised in your religious imagination that GOD is in the Heaven, above all of the other stars and planets; and yet HE sends His Spirit down here to your hearts and minds; even so send I MY Spirit to the children of men, from this TABERNACLE in which I live. It is equivalently the same.

Now I would further like to say (FATHER arises from His seat, and continuing says):

PEACE, EVERYONE:

There are those who even say, "If FATHER DIVINE is GOD, why is it HE allows so much bloodshed? Why is it HE allows so many wars and race riots and such as that?" Nevertheless, as it was, and as it is with your imaginary GOD, if GOD is GOD from your imaginary version, why is it, GOD does not stop these things when you pray to HIM?

The Individual: HE is Ruler of this World.

FATHER: I say, "Why is it GOD does not stop those things when you pray to HIM?"

The Individual: GOD created this world with one of His Angels, but Satan rules the world and makes gangsters. That is why HE sent HIS Son.

FATHER: Yes, but I AM come this time, and shall take the rule out of that one which you call Satan's hand. That is exactly what I AM doing now. I AM breaking down every idol, I AM casting out every foe; I AM bringing mankind into subjection. That is why they are stirred from center to circumference, because I AM doing what they said GOD would do. I AM just doing it.

All of the praying to the imaginary God, that kind of Religion has kept the under-privileged down-trodden until this day. Men such as Mr. Ellender whom you all may have read or heard of, will send such missionaries as you to Africa to teach the people something, to China to teach the people something—to the Chinese, and to Japan to teach the people something, and to others whom they consider to be unintelligent; but what do they teach them? They teach them to keep GOD in the imaginary Heaven, so HE cannot come down here to prohibit them from committing crime and legalizing crime; but I have come right here on the earth. I have come and I shall stop those things with or without a BODY.

It is absolutely immaterial to ME whether I have a BODY or not; with or without a BODY, I will stop those things, but as long as the mortal-minded religions will allow the people to continue to keep their minds in Heaven some place, and "the other fellow" have all power down here,—the reason I say, "the other fellow"—you may be a stranger, I say "the other fellow" commonly known by the Religions, "the devil"—now so long as you and others will keep "the other fellow" down here ruling the earth and put GOD away up in Heaven, where he cannot protect you, why, then you will always have miseries and sufferings among the people; but MY Followers are living in splendor, with the Abundance of all things, because they recognize GOD'S ACTUAL PRESENCE.

This was the Mission of HIM of Whom you say You are serving. "His Name shall be called IMMANUEL, being interpreted GOD is with us." I merely came to fulfill your own Christian Religion, you see. GOD is with us; to convince you GOD is with the children of Men. They were driven from GOD'S PRESENCE in the Garden of Eden, but CHRIST came and died that you might have the right to the Tree of Life.

I have not denied the advent of the CHRIST from the Jesus point of view. This was an advent to bring to man, the recognition of GOD'S ACTUAL PRESENCE.

Now this is actually fulfilling the Scripture; "He is present with you," and if you believe in GOD'S ACTUAL PRESENCE and disbelieve in the imaginary GOD, as said the Scripture, "GOD is not a God afar off, but GOD is a GOD at hand."

This was predicted in the old Bible even before Jesus the CHRIST came. It says, "GOD is not a God afar off, but GOD is a God at hand." It was only through the misconception of the human Religions that they were led erroneously by their false imaginations that GOD was far away in some imaginary Heaven; but John caught the mystery concerning this of which we are now speaking, and said:

"I saw a New Heaven and a New earth, for the first Heaven and the first earth are passed away:

"And I, John, saw the Holy City, new Jerusalem, coming down from God out of Heaven, prepared as a bride adorned for her husband; and I heard a great voice out of Heaven saying, Behold, the TABERNACLE OF GOD is with men, and HE will dwell with them, and they shall be His people, and GOD HIMSELF," no longer just the Son, nor the Angels, nor the Spirit, but "GOD HIMSELF shall be with them, and shall be their GOD." "And they shall be His people."

Now this is the "revelationic" prediction of John in the Book of Revelation —the twenty-first chapter. Read it for yourself. Now if you read this chapter carefully with meditation, and pray to your Jesus and be true to HIM, HE as ME, will tell you that "I AM HE."

The Individual: How long did it take You to come down from Heaven?

FATHER: Where is the Heaven? Tell ME how far is it?

The Persistent Individual: FATHER DIVINE, how long did it take YOU to come down from Heaven?

FATHER: I asked you a question. If you tell ME where Heaven and what is Heaven, then I can answer the question.

The Individual: But YOU know my thoughts.

FATHER: Naturally I do. Spiritually I do, Intellectually I do. Socially I do, and from every point expressible I do. Hence, if you be silent, if you wish to ask a question, and will ask ME in your heart, I will answer it.

[Editor:] (And so this dialogue ended with much information to the followers and others who were present, but little to the questioner, as her mind was set and fixed and closed to all reasonable understanding. For this, LORD, we thank THEE. FATHER speaks again as follows:)

PEACE EVERYONE:

("Peace, FATHER DEAR!" replied the audience responsively.)

(Father Divine Continued:)

Since there is no one speaking, I will further say for the benefit of My hearers and those who will get My Message the universe over, it matters not what the different Religions and the politicians say, to try to keep you in bondage of the fear of some other place, beneath the ground, and the fear of some other place far above all of the other planets. *You are all substantiated.*

Men try to use Religion to keep you in bondage, to enslave you, but I came and have truly emancipated you. I would not give five cents for a God who could not help me here on the earth, for such a God is not a God at hand. He is only an imagination. It is a false delusion—trying to make you think you had just as well go ahead and suffer and be enslaved and be lynched and everything else here, and after a while you are going to Heaven some place. If GOD cannot prepare Heaven here for you, you are not going anywhere.

We shall have a RIGHTEOUS GOVERNMENT right down here on earth. All of the inhabitants of the earth shall recognize the ACTUAL PRESENCE of GOD, who will bring themselves into subjection to HIM, and none shall prevent HIM. I thank you.

V

Platform of Rights: Overcoming Racial Discrimination

Although Father Divine's followers in the Peace Mission Movement continually affirm that they recognize no race because "God hath made of one blood all races of men," there has always been a strong emphasis on overcoming racial discrimination. The success of integration is one more "Miracle" attesting to the charisma of Father Divine.

From *New Day* references and testimonies often heard in his churches it is apparent that Father Divine had been a foe of racial discrimination long before he had a following, and more than once had faced lynch mobs in the South. The trial before Judge Smith was treated by his lawyers as a case of racial discrimination. Defending the Movement's right to stay in Sayville, they argued that racial prejudice had instigated the original attacks on the religious ceremonies in the Divine community. Newspapers bore out that contention. Followers and sympathizers supported the allegation. Eugene Del Mar's letter to the *New York Times*, reproduced in Chapter II, also emphasized the antiracist aspect of the Movement and the total resistance to discrimination which it preached.

The constituency of the Movement has been integrated at least since the middle of the Sayville period (1919–1932). Older members who still testify to healings, visions, and conversion in this period are of all complexions, and certainly represent several so-called races, no matter whether we use the layman's or the anthropologist's definition of race.

During the middle 1930s a Righteous Government Movement was organized by followers of Father Divine. A convention in New York City, attended by persons from many states and some foreign countries, culminated in the adoption of the "Righteous Government Platform of Father Divine's Peace Mission Movement." The Movement still adheres to this Platform's central "planks" calling for equal treatment of all races and persons in the United States. The Platform is still read and discussed at meetings of the Church in Philadelphia and elsewhere, where members testify to their achievements in implementing the planks. Each issue of the *New Day* reports on progress in race relations all over the world.

With respect to race and color, the Platform states:

> We do not mean to say that men can be made righteous, just and truthful by law, for "It is not by power or by might but by My Spirit, says The Lord." It was not the law that caused millions of people to return stolen goods, to pay up old bills, to become honest, competent and true and be law-abiding citizens when they were just the opposite before they knew Father Divine; it was His Spirit and Mind entering into them. However, the time is at hand for righteousness, justice and truth to be legalized, and for those that are unrighteous, unjust and untrue and will not observe the righteousness of the law, to be designated as criminals. Therefore we demand the following:[1]

PLANKS

1

Immediate repeal of all laws, ordinances, rules, and regulations, local and national, in the United States and elsewhere, that have been passed contrary to the Spirit and meaning of the Constitution of the United States and its amendments.

2

Immediate legislation in every state in the Union, and all other states and countries, making it a crime to discriminate in any public place against any individual on account of race, creed, or color; abolishing all segregated neighborhoods in cities and towns, making it a crime for landlords or hotels to refuse tenants on such grounds; abolishing all segregated schools, and colleges, and all segregated areas in churches, theatres, public conveyances, and other public places.

3

Legislation making it a crime for any newspaper, magazine, or other publication to use segregated or slang words referring to race, creed or color of any individual or group or write abusively concerning any.

8

Legislation to abolish lynching and outlaw members of lynch mobs, in all states and countries.

Legislation making it a violation of the law, to withhold any kind of classification of work from any Civil Service employee on account of race, creed or color, provided he or she is qualified to do such work.

11

Legislation making it a crime for any employer to discharge an employee, even through a subordinate, when even circumstantial evidence can be introduced to show that it was on account of race, creed or color.

12

Legislation establishing a maximum fee for all labor union memberships, causing them to accept all qualified applicants and give them equal privileges regardless of race, creed, color or classification; also providing that any labor union which limits the hours and days of work per week, must guarantee at least that much work per week to its members, and if it calls a strike, pay its members while they are out of work, the full amount they are demanding from the employers; otherwise all obligations for dues must cease.

13

Immediate repeal of all laws and ordinances, governmental rules and regulations requiring individuals to designate themselves of being of a race, creed or color in signing any kind of papers; this to apply especially to immigration, citizenship, passport or legal papers.

14

Legislation making it unlawful for employers of skilled or unskilled, technical or professional help, to have different wage scales or salaries for what they term different races, creeds or colors; or to discriminate in any way in the hiring of help.

Three other sets of planks concern economics, education, and politics. Eight out of fourteen planks deal in some way with race. Of twelve planks within the economic set one deals with equal treatment:

> Laws to be altered so that Equal Opportunity is allowed to all, that every
> worker be allowed access to the land, to the tools and materials needed for
> the carrying out of his individual talent, for the welfare of himself and of
> society.

The two planks of the political section are prefaced by a long statement by Father
Divine affirming that politicians who vote according to his principles have his
spirit whether they know it or not, and that they should be supported no matter
what their party:

> The followers of Father Divine belong to no one political party or organi-
> zation though they may cooperate with many, under Father's leading, in
> the cause of Righteousness, Justice and Truth. They vote for the candidate
> who is best fitted for office, regardless of his political affiliation, if they are
> convinced he will deal justly with Truth and Righteousness. If his public or
> private life have ever shown prejudice, bigotry, or discrimination; vice,
> crime or opposition to the reign of CHRIST; or his record shows tenden-
> cies of selfishness, graft, greed or political corruption, they don't want him
> in office regardless of his promises. A very efficient research department is
> maintained in the Righteous Government Program, to gather this infor-
> mation and record the stand of the officials of our city, state and Federal
> governments on the various issues, and this information is available to all.[2]

The two political planks call for equal suffrage and equal opportunity for governmental employment for qualified persons.

> 1
>
> That all candidates, including candidates for president be nominated en-
> tirely by the people, and that they be required to meet specified require-
> ments, to prove their qualifications for office, not as politicians but tech-
> nical experts.
>
> 2
>
> Immediate abandonment of the political patronage system, and appoint-
> ment of all Civil Service employees strictly according to their qualifications
> and service, and their standing on the list, without regard to party, race,
> creed or color, and without intervention of political leaders.

The preface to the Educational Section states:

Through the educational program of the Righteous Government Department, those of the masses who are not already qualified are being qualified to pass the literacy tests, to register and to vote intelligently, to pass Civil Service examinations, and to fill any offices they might be called to fill. They are attending the evening schools in such numbers, the local schools in the City of New York have not been sufficient to accommodate them and extra facilities have been provided. In the Kingdom and its extensions, private schools have been established under the direction of regular teachers, to care for the needs of those who are otherwise engaged during the school hours, and there are many such schools throughout the country.[3]

The Educational Section continues:

For the advancement of real education and culture among the people, we request the following:

1

The doors of all educational institutions to be open and free to all for universal education, with equal rights for all to technical and professional teaching.

2

The abolishing in all educational institutions, and from books used for educational purposes in such institutions, of all references to racial conflicts or differences, and national glory through military feats, etc., with legislation making it a misdemeanor for any educator to teach such to his classes.[4]

Two amendments bear directly or indirectly on interracial and intergroup understanding.

Section on Principles. No. 8-A

Legislation imposing the penalty for first degree murder[5] on all members of lynch-mobs killing or fatally injuring any person, together with a fine of ten to twenty dollars to be paid by the county wherein the lynching occurs, to the estate of the injured or deceased person.

Appended to this plank in 1938 was a statement by Father Divine concerning the Costigan–Wagner Anti-Lynching Bill, up for debate in Congress at that time.

I just wish to say in reference to the "Anti-lynching Bill," if this is not inserted in it, it is not severe enough. This of which I am about to Say, was and is—if one person will murder a man without the law, he is subject to punishment to the extent of being termed a murderer. If two men will commit the same crime, many of them have been charged as a murderer and received the penalty of the same. This should be in the "Anti-lynching Bill." Every man in the lynch mob should be convicted as a murderer—not one alone, but every one, for they are all murderers, and if we would tolerate it they would continue to indulge in wholesale murder by getting together by the hundreds and thousands. Therefore, I Say, a lynch mob does murder. It is an organization, an organized body of murderers. Every member of a lynch mob that would lynch a man should go to the same place wheresoever men are supposed to go when they commit that crime.[6]

In introducing the second amendment, adding plank 3A to the Education Section, Father Divine said:

For the purpose of bringing all men together, I came to convert all the systems. There shall be no division after a while in language. There shall be ONE LANGUAGE! Now isn't that Wonderful! Firstly it was essential to eradicate and abolish divisions among us as races, creeds and colors supposedly, but for the Perfect Work to be accomplished there will not be divisions in systems, languages, tongues nor people, for they all shall understand each other with the one language we are speaking.

Now I do not say, especially, it must be broken English as I am Speaking, but whatever language Divine LOVE and GOD'S Omniscience finds sufficient and quite efficient for the purpose, will be adopted, and all peoples shall talk it. I am not especially trying to justify the American language as broken English, neither am I especially trying to adopt it as the international language, but as a Representative of RIGHTEOUSNESS, TRUTH and JUSTICE, I am seeking a language to be spoken that will be of more effect, and more suitable for all nations, languages, tongues and people.[7]

The plank is:

The adoption of a universal language by all nations, languages, tongues and peoples—all governments to assist in establishing it by including it in the courses of study in all public schools and colleges.

The Movement has adopted English as its language; followers in all countries seek to learn it and take great pride in their ability to speak "Father's language." When they visit from Germany or Switzerland, their testimonies at meetings and banquets are in English. The *New Day* was published in a German edition[8] for many years but this seems to have been discontinued, perhaps to stress the value of studying the paper in English.

Sermons, communions, and Wedding Anniversary services taped to be sent out to member meetings are, of course, in English and are a great incentive to the foreign follower to grasp the language. Besides the language, the whole ideology of the United States Constitution and the Bill of Rights is urged upon followers in other lands who display American flags at all their meetings and sing "WE are all true, good, Americans." Some who migrated to the United States participate actively in the churches, hotels, and "homes" in Philadelphia. They seek to live as close to "the Body" (of Father Divine) as possible. The writer became aware of several such individuals in his participation with the Movement[9] and there must be many more.

In Australia, Switzerland, Germany, Canada, and England the groups have found it difficult to "enact the bill" (the Movement's phrase for integration) because there are so few people of other so-called races in the area. Letters from these groups make a special reference to someone of another race and give Father thanks for the privilege of having them there. A visitor from the Canal Zone spoke to one of the observers for the study about the thrill it gave them in their Canal Zone church to have a follower of the "lighter complexion" visit them so they could "enact the bill." The emphasis on equality, she reported, was a strong factor in Father Divine's appeal in her country, where segregation in the whole society extends to churches.

Immediately after the Righteous Government Platform was published, Congress started passing federal emergency legislation almost weekly. The Peace Movement's stand on economic legislation in the Economic Section had endorsed even more extensive government control than had the socialists in certain areas, but much less in others. Collective ownership and systematic abstention from government welfare schemes, still practiced in the Movement today, was advocated and practiced by the true followers at this time.

The Principles planks, most of which dealt with intergroup relations, included one (number 5) which called for "repeal of all laws or ordinances providing for compulsory insurance, employers' liability, public liability, or any other form of compulsory insurance." It was felt that dependence on such economic devices indicated a distrust of God's protection and power.

Righteous Government Forums, organized to implement the Platform, were reported in the *New Day* at many places in Harlem, Brooklyn, Ulster County, New York, and the West Coast throughout the 1930s. Guest speakers of all denominations and parties and representatives of many "isms" were allowed to speak on a wide range of topics. In the *New Day* of March 10, 1938, various items such as these appeared, with economics and the race issue as their two central themes.[10]

RIGHTEOUS GOVERNMENT NEWS—ANGELS FROM COLORADO VISIT OAKLAND, CALIFORNIA

We thank Father for the wonderful way HE has blessed HIS work and progress around the Bay Region. Several outstanding guest speakers have appeared before the forum. One, Mr. George Towne, a representative of the W.P.A. Education Program, spoke on FATHER'S PLATFORM in connection with current events.

On February 20th a lovely group of angels from Santa Cruz and Colorado visited us, told of their wonderful experiences, and sang many new songs that FATHER had given them. There was a lovely gathering of FATHER'S angels at 821 Pacific Street, San Francisco, on that afternoon, to rejoice over the victory that FATHER had won by causing Senator Ellender to read many Planks of HIS RIGHTEOUS GOVERNMENT PLATFORM before the Senate during the filibuster. At 952 Eighth St., Oakland, there was a most glorious meeting in the evening. Many strangers were present, and the auditorium was filled to overflowing. The vibrations rang high. We thank FATHER for these marvelous blessings.

FATHER blessed a group of angels from the Bay Region to go to Fresno to spread the Glad Tidings that GOD, FATHER DIVINE is in the land.

FATHER has a few angels there, who are thanking HIM to establish a Peace Mission.

JUNIORS AT HIGH FALLS[11]

The Junior Department of the Righteous Government Movement of High Falls holds meetings every night.

The little angels are very ambitious and enthusiastic in their study of the Righteous Government Platform and can recite many of the planks from memory.

At their usual meeting on Friday, March 4, the little children presented their program, expressing in songs recitals; and a short skit was given which stressed the significance of honesty and sincerity in getting schools lessons. A few letters which were written to Senator Ellender were read from the Congressional Records. There were several interesting discussions during the course of the evening.

PROFIT SHARING INVESTIGATION DISCUSSED AT SPEAKERS' BUREAU

For the benefit of those who may find it difficult to keep informed about the various measures being discussed in Congress, the bureau is taking it as its duty to bring these measures before the masses each Sunday afternoon at 4:30 P.M.

Feb. 27th the subject was: "A Resolution to Investigate Profit Sharing Enterprises." The bill was read and explained thoroughly and then left open for general discussion.

It was said that the investigation was suggested because the government felt that many corporations were claiming to be on the profit sharing basis in order to evade taxes. Also it was believed the Senate should get a report from the employees of these enterprises, to verify the statements in their books and the books should show how much of the profits were being shared with the employees.

We know it is the Spirit of FATHER that is urging this investigation, because it is His Mission here to uncover all unrighteousness.

ECONOMICS AND LYNCHING DISCUSSED AT HEADQUARTERS FORUM

To the allegation that followers give all they have to FATHER, Andrew Peace replied by telling what he had when he came to the Movement. He said that he had a pair of pants needing patches, soleless shoes, and kept a roof over his head by threats, as he could not pay the rent—some sickness and a lot of sin. Now he is partner in a store, prosperous and healthy.

Dr. Broadman read the plank in the Platform about the government taking over the farms and factories. He said that was a definite policy of government cooperation (or interference) in business. He cited uses and abuses of such policy; favoring its proper administration.

Statistics pertinent to lynching were read by Grace Lemmon. Virginia's anti-lynching law has prevented all lynchings in that state since it was enacted in 1928. Many southern papers favored the anti-lynch bill against which Senator Ellender and others filibustered recently. Many papers carried favorable editorials on the bill which received the greatest favorable response of any issue in recent years.

Mr. Nardiello, of Newark, was present and spoke eloquently on the benefits FATHER DIVINE is bringing to communities in which His Movement is active.

References to Senator Ellender and the Anti-Lynching Bill have to do with a filibuster he was conducting against it. In order to ridicule Father Divine who was sponsoring a letter campaign for the bill, Ellender read into the *Congressional Record* the whole Righteous Government Platform, criticizing many of its planks as he read them.[12] Father Divine called Ellender "a little dog baying at the moon" and for many months after spoke of the printing of the Platform in the *Congressional Record* as an act brought about through an enemy, showing that Father Divine's spirit was in Washington and in Congress. It proved that Father Divine as God could use even the most prejudiced enemy for His purposes. Like the reversal of the Sayville trial verdict and Judge Smith's death, the publicity from Senator Ellender's speech is still cited as an example of Father Divine's supernatural power. Songs sung in Movement gatherings still allude to this incident.

Up to this point two ways of dealing with race relations had contributed to Father Divine's charisma: actual integration within the Movement and support of civil rights legislation forbidding many types of discriminatory practices.

A dramatic event occurred in 1946 when Father Divine was married to a blond Canadian follower, Edna Rose Ritchings. Having grown up in the Movement in Vancouver, Canada, and having come to Philadelphia as a young girl to become a Rosebud and one of the Secretaries under the new name of Sweet Angel, she soon, and surprisingly, became the second wife of Father Divine. He explained that she was a reincarnation of his first wife, Peninah, who had become dissatisfied with her large, heavy bodily form. He had finally let her "pass," after years during which she had asked for that privilege.[13]

Announcement of the marriage, first to the press and then to the followers, may have resulted in some defections from the Movement, but the membership did not drop off appreciably. If there were those who, despite their acceptance of integrated living, could not accept symbolic interracial marriage, this event was bound to separate them from their Lord. Father Divine made it very clear that this was a symbolic, spiritual marriage, never to be consummated in the worldly physical sense.

Every Wedding Anniversary, the twenty-ninth day of April, has become a greater feast day. Now the most important event of the church year, it requires weeks of preparation and "reviews" all over the world.

It is described as "an international, Interracial, Universal Holiday," commemorating the Holy Marriage of FATHER DIVINE and MOTHER DIVINE, symbolizing Christ and the Church and the Birth of the Church United and reviews of April 29th are celebrated around the world throughout the year.[14]

These services, Communion Banquets, and visitations to the new or improved properties in Philadelphia attract the faithful from all Movement churches. An afternoon at Woodmont on such occasions brings followers together from as far as California in the plane that is chartered annually. Twenty-five to fifty manage to make a yearly trip. Swiss, German and Australian followers often arrive for a visit. Detroit, Chicago, New Jersey, Connecticut, and New York City contribute perhaps as many as four hundred. A scattering of followers and "strangers" may come from almost anywhere in the United States or the world, but the greatest number are always resident followers in the several-million-dollars' worth of hotels, apartment houses and mansions in Philadelphia, New York City, and Newark, New Jersey.[15]

Since Sweet Angel became Mother Divine, she has been given increasingly greater respect. When Father Divine ceased to speak in public, in 1960, Mother presided as spokesman for the Movement, passing each item at the banquet to Father for his blessing. She still functions as hostess and in her own name issues invitations to visitors to speak. Praises are now addressed to Father-Mother Divine as she assumes an ever more important role in the Peace Mission Movement's public activities.

To many this "Holy Marriage" is a final proof that Father Divine has charisma, for only God "could overcome the prejudice of 'mortal mind' in such a marvelous way."

VI

Overcoming the Depression

Father Divine always represented his Movement as a practical program dealing with problems of life on this earth. He had no patience with pie-in-the-sky religion nor with a heaven in some imaginary place. He preached a heaven on earth in which every individual has the same rights: independence, a job, self-respect, and the recognition of Father Divine as God.

The message preached after his triumphant return from prison to an audience of listeners in depression Harlem can be summarized in quotations taken from Father Divine's thousands of talks. He warned that politicians and some religious leaders might use threats of hell and rewards in heaven to mislead their followers and lull them into acceptance of inequality in this world:

> Men try to use religion to keep you in bondage, to enslave you, but I came and truly emancipated you . . . it matters not what the different religions and politicians say, to try to keep you in bondage of the fear of some other place, beneath the ground, and the fear of some other place far above all the other planets . . . I would not give five cents for a God who could not help me here on earth, for such a God is not a God at hand. He is only an imagination. It is a false delusion—trying to make you think you had just as well go ahead and be enslaved and be lynched and everything else here, and after a while you are going to a heaven some place. If GOD cannot prepare Heaven for you here, you are not going anywhere.[1]

Although there had been a "holy community" gathered about Father Divine, followers who actually lived together and were in constant contact with him, the "heaven" which he was to create was always projected beyond this group. The whole earth was to have a righteous government, if it would recognize the actual presence of God—a Spirit available everywhere if men would but "follow the statutes of God."[2]

Grandiose and idealistic as the ideology of the Movement was, the actual practice of these values was opportunistic, specific, and very personal. Such declarations as "the principles of Americanism, Brotherhood, Christianity, Democracy, Buddhisim and True Judaism are synonymous," expressed ideals of equality and economic independence. But realizing that everyone was not yet aware of or willing to accept such a definition of the righteous government (or the Kingdom of Heaven on Earth) members of the group described themselves as "examplars" for the future. They held that if everyone waited for the other fellow to start living righteously the world would continue to be in the control of "the other fellow." Explanations for the unrighteousness found in the world revolved around the concepts of "the other fellow" and of mortal mind. In Father Divine's words:

> I say "the other fellow" commonly known by the religions as "the devil" has power down here as long as the mortal-minded religious people will allow the people to continue to keep their minds in Heaven some place. As long . . . as you will keep "the other fellow" down here ruling the earth and put God away up in Heaven, where He cannot protect you, why, then you will always have miseries and sufferings among the people; but My followers are living in splendor, with the abundance of all things, because they recognize GOD'S ACTUAL PRESENCE.[3]

For each individual the way to overcome the devil was to behave according to the dicta of Father Divine, speaking as God. Only the mortal mind would allow the devil to rule.

As in all religious movements, various appeals evoked support and loyalty from followers with diverse needs. As a social type, the economic and socially underprivileged have always been very prominent in this group. Father Divine emphasized that "the religions" did not serve the people, but preserved and even encouraged acceptance of "low-rated positions":

> All of the praying to the imaginary God of that kind of religion has kept the under-privileged down-trodden until this day. Men such as Mr. Ellender . . . will send . . . missionaries to Africa to teach the people something, to China . . . and to Japan . . . to teach the people something, and to others they consider to be unintelligent; but what do they teach them? They teach them to keep God in the imaginary Heaven, so He cannot come down here to prohibit them from committing crime and legalizing crime.[4]

The economic base of life was clearly recognized as essential. As in the Protestant Ethic, work, self-support, savings and investments, and the sanctity of property were highly extolled. A type of asceticism was practiced which partly accounted for the accumulation of capital for productive purposes.

Although newspaper and popular articles throughout the depression emphasized bizarre and circuslike aspects of the Movement and especially of Father Divine, it was his service to the underprivileged and the socially alienated which developed his solid base of charisma.

Ever since the breakup of the feudal relationship established under slavery, the Afro–American had faced the problem of unemployment. Untrained for competition in many occupations—or, if he was trained, the last to be hired and the first to be laid off—and caught in the disintegration of the cotton economy of the South and not yet integrated into the new urban culture of the North or South, he could find no solution for his economic problem. Middle-class minority group members who had found some economic security lost touch with the lowest economic segment of the population and could be of little help there.[5]

It will be recalled that the first service rendered by the Rev. M. J. Divine was an employment service, followed by a room and board service. The same arrangements persist to this day, but on a more complicated and sophisticated basis.

When the Movement shifted to the city in the 1930s properties were rented or bought; some were called churches or Peace Missions, others were exclusively rooming houses. Purchased by pooling followers' funds, the properties were held in the followers' names. But all were dedicated to Father Divine; his advice was sought and taken in the conduct of these missions and businesses. Some followers started small businesses either as individuals or as "co-workers."

Father Divine made no secret of the fact that he was supported by the grateful followers who ran these businesses. Although in court he could honestly deny personal ownership of the business end of his Movement, in public meetings he often made such statements as:

> See what I am doing for you. You can come to these different auditoriums and dining rooms and follow ME around wheresoever you will—not one penny have you been requested to give ME, nor any other individual connected with ME, unless you get more than that penny's worth, for the penny you are requested to give—for food, for shelter, or for raiment. From the dress shops and other places, I have told you and I have shown you, if you cannot get things as reasonable and more reasonable in the dress shops under the Spirit and Guidance of the Peace Mission, go elsewhere and buy. I have shown you conclusively, MY work must be absolutely independent, it must be competent and must be reliable and it must be profitable. By working on the cooperative basis it can be profitable and can be much more profitable than others.
>
> You can earn more and clear more than others by cooperation and harmo-

nization, and by MY Spirit and MY Presence and MY INFINITE BLESSINGS.

Groceries and all the places of business, those places that all claim to be representing ME,—if they cannot and will not give you more than what any others can and will give you, do not patronize them, do not give them your patronage; for MY Spirit has come to give the best and always the best for the least.

All of the different places of business, if they do not choose to live and do according to MY Teaching, even those under MY Personal Jurisdiction; if they will allow some other individual to slip in in connection with them and cause them to deviate from MY Teaching and will not give the public or the consumer more than . . . elsewhere . . . do not buy from them. . . . And I am talking about myself, if you would but know it. . . . I am trying to keep MY blessings from coming to ME.[6]

In the next statement the mystery of Father Divine's support, which he in other places and occasions used as a sign of Godlike power, was spelled out clearly: his followers supported him from their earnings. There was no mystery. Like any minister, he was supported by those to whom he preached, and in proportion to their faith in the value of his message. The fact that the newspapers contributed to the myth by exaggerating his wealth and its mysterious sources probably added to the charismatic quality of Father Divine and the Movement. And, indeed, to many followers who had never dared to work for themselves before, but found self-assurance in the Movement to do it, there was charisma at work:

For when MY immediate followers under MY Personal Spiritual Jurisdiction are blessed, automatically I am blessed; for they will give ME such things as may be desired by me apparently. These things that I may apparently need they will give me. . . . I desire those things that would come to ME to come through MY method and through MY Plan only, and that must be a method of absolute honesty, competence and truth, that you might know definitely it is not coming through graft nor through greed.[7]

Father Divine furnished both bread and joy. The religious services and parades and outings were the joy. The "bread" was furnished by providing for three needs not being met for a sizable portion of the population from 1932 till the war boom of the 1940s. These needs were shelter, food, and clothing, and the immediate means of achieving these was work which Father Divine took the credit for creating. He sought to instill in his followers respect for themselves as efficient workers deserving a fair wage:

You should not go on the job to idle, to loaf nor to do any such thing as that.

You should give the world the best you have and expect the best to come back to you.

If you go on a job you should know what you are going for and demand a living wage, for you have to pay for what you eat and drink and wear. If you do not someone else does. Just because God has arranged so you can live on much less than before you saw Me, this does not say that you should go out and enslave yourselves.

You should earn a living wage. People are trying to get you to work for a dollar a day—it is an outrage, it is ridiculous.[8]

Even though they could live for five dollars a week in the "extensions," he told them they should receive pay commensurate with their skills and occupations; twenty-five, thirty, or forty dollars a week would not be too much to expect as wages for their skills. They could use the money to pay off old debts and they "must make ready for the advancement of a better living condition in our community and in our surroundings."

Once he had collected a group about him, housed in extensions and the church buildings, he showed that work was available, if not to be found in the outside world then in maintaining the services of the organization as cooks, waitresses, seamstresses, and mechanics.

A would-be follower who was a reluctant worker would be given a warning and, disregarding it, he might find himself without a spiritual or material home:

To those who come here from time to time, and through My condescension we take them in as strangers, some of them, and they say they want to work; some, when you give it to them, they just do not want it. They do not want to work. It is for this cause it is even detrimental, in a way of speaking, to lift some out of the gutters and out of the lowest parts of expression to the height of heaven, and give them access to and in these blessings; for the majority of them do not appreciate them.

If the sister to whom I am speaking, just will not work, why, if you see she does not have a home, you may know why; because if you have your health and your strength you should desire to be competent and true and be independent. Even though I have given and may from time to time give people homes—if you want to live in sin, or whatsoever you want to do out of Me and away from Me and Mine, that is your privilege to do so.[9]

An employment service placed workers in jobs; those who started their own businesses were assured that their activity would encourage a real revolution in the commercial world. In April 1938 twenty-six businesses (apart from the many "residences") were operated by the followers; by 1942 the number had grown to sixty-three businesses and many more residences. Small as they were, run by one to six people—restaurants, groceries, fish markets, laundries, men's clothing shops, women's clothing shops, shoe repair shops, shoeshining, trucking—and sometimes quite ephemeral, they did prove to many followers that they could work for themselves with God's help. During the war years many disappeared, so that in September 1956 there were only three more than in 1938. But Father Divine had accomplished the miracle of putting people to work; while the war years furnished enough work for all, Father's charisma had long since been validated by the depression experience.[10]

The depression-challenging message that these businesses preached, according to Divine word, was this:

> We shall have higher wages for the working people as well as for those who are not classed as working people. We shall have higher wages for the laborers, the employees and we shall be more successful in business by lowering the prices of commodities and selling merchandise at the smallest prices possible. The volume of business will be so increased and so immensed until, by fast turning over for cash, you will earn more yearly and even monthly than you could dare to do with high prices and yet you will be a blessing to the community and a blessing to the individual customer. We are looking forward for a great change to take place in our commercial system as well as in the capitalistic system.[11]

During the 1930s restaurants run by followers were required by Father Divine's direct command to offer meals priced at ten and fifteen cents. In his sermons he made frequent reference to the thousands he was feeding free at his banquets and his restaurants. Since it was possible for followers to make contributions for food (although these were payment for services received rather than contributions), the income from feeding may have been substantial. According to Father Divine's theory, the workers in these restaurants and banquets were the true followers who had abandoned the expensive way of life outside the extensions, and hence could live on five dollars a week. They received what amounted to a subsistence wage. Eliminating the largest part of the labor cost thus made inexpensive meals feasible.

Obviously, one of the reasons for the apparent financial success of the Movement has been the constant reiteration of the ideology of the Godliness of work and of Divine asceticism.

Operation of apartments, "homes," and hotels has been the most successful economic activity. Listed in the appendix are forty-five properties which house some of the followers. Even buildings designated as churches contain sleeping quarters. The Yonkers mansion, the Tarrytown estate, and Woodmont furnish living quarters for a number of followers. Several hotels—for example, the Riviera in Newark and the Tracy and Lorraine in Philadelphia—are open to the public, so that hotelkeeping has become an income-producing occupation.

While these properties provide occupations in maintenance, several house older and retired people, furnishing employment to practical nurses and others.

Catering became a major activity of a number of followers, since many residents procured their food through the restaurants or at the "communion table." In the larger hotels, cafeterias, open to the public, are maintained. Such hotels as the Lorraine prepare and serve dinners for outside organizations who rent meeting rooms. Regulations forbidding smoking and liquor may limit the variety of organizations availing themselves of this service.

Besides the nurses who care for old people in several of the homes, others are members of an association called United Peace Mission Nurses who work wherever they find acceptable patients. Despite Father Divine's emphasis on divine healing he admonished his followers at the Movement's Interracial Nurses' Training School in Newark:

> Do not be confined to the meager profession of practical nurse. I called for trained nurses! I called for perfection in medical skill from every angle expressible. Those who are qualified and those who are not qualified, I have called for it and we must have it!

> Go to any school to get more information if it does not cause you to sacrifice your economic security! But if you must sacrifice your economic security, it is better to have an economic security than be, I might say, intellectually perfect and be economically or from a monetary point of view defunct.[12]

In other words, he urged his listeners, buy only the education you can afford. The Peace Mission nurse is to:

> carry out every order given by the physician, realizing her patient's faith in him. Nevertheless, she will silently and persistently retain her own religious convictions in her practice, and will know how to mentally and spiritually discriminate between what to absorb and what not to absorb—what to accept and what not to accept. . . . She should forever be conscious of the finite knowledge of man and the infinite Wisdom of God. She should know

deep down in her heart that the extent of man's knowledge is a temporary cure; but the Infinite Spirit of GOD, FATHER DIVINE, heals and makes one whole again. . . . She will not try to preach Christ so much in words, but she will hold the torch high in deeds, actions and service, so that all can see the Light, followed by her good works, and glorify our FATHER in Heaven on earth.[13]

The practicality in financial matters which marks much of the philosophy of the Movement is illustrated here. First, although the value of education is extolled, caution is also urged not to bankrupt oneself in seeking intellectual perfection— economic security is the greater value.

These remarks illustrate both the practical approach to financial matters and caution in dealing with conflicting, worldly medical views which are characteristic of the Movement. A deeper conflict between spiritual healing and mundane medical care runs throughout the history of the Movement.[14] Sickness and death among the followers is held to be the result of "sin," "the carnal mind," "following the other fellow," "prejudiced behavior," or simply not allowing Father Divine to control one's mentality. Medicine is for those who will not "let Father in."

At any rate, those who wished to earn a living and do a service to man by nursing had Father Divine's assurance that they were humanitarians at heart "with love for fellowmen, regardless of race, creed or color." They in turn pledged:

Oh God, our heavenly Father Divine, the Great Physician, the Life Giver, we pledge these hearts, minds and bodies—that Thou has cleansed and purged—as a living sacrifice to God and man.

We acknowledge we are as empty pitchers before a full fountain. We are depending on Your Holy Spirit to make us true ministering Spirits.

We promise to be loyal, patient, kind, true and obedient, meek and sweet. We will minister to the needs of all humanity regardless of race, creed or color, so help us God.[15]

The reiteration of self-support was often accompanied by Father Divine's warning that God would punish those who refused to work to the best of their ability. His denunciations in public meetings were a strong influence toward reform or separation. Coworkers and roommates of the offender had an obligation to put moral pressure on him to assume his share of "family burdens" or return to the "world." Drones have not lasted long in the Kingdom of Father Divine.[16]

True followers serve a trial in the economic realm, must pay up all back debts, re-

imburse stolen funds, cancel insurance, refuse public assistance, forego workmen's compensation, and destroy (at personal loss) any counterfeit money in
their possession. This almost certainly exerted a strong selective process, weeding out prospective applicants not willing to subordinate immediate economic
needs to their belief in Father Divine.

Followers who acted on these demands, as many did, generated favorable publicity for Father Divine. They reinforced existing members' belief in his charisma,
since they felt and testified that only an extraordinary being could have reversed
their feelings about debts, crimes, insurance, or government aid.

After 1932, newspapers across the country began to report conscience payments
ranging from a few cents for trolley fare to thousands of dollars in unpaid income
taxes. The *New Day* often ran page after page of reproductions of letters acknowledging payments to hospitals, department stores, bureaus of public assistance, landlords, and former employers. This practice still continues. Recipients
of the funds were told that belief in Father Divine's divinity was responsible for
the funds being paid and asked for their acknowledgment.

Two letters from the 1930s, and one more recent, illustrate how Father Divine
developed his charisma from such acts of recompense.

The first is a letter to a follower from the recipient of a payment:

> My dear Wonderful:
>
> I am in receipt of your letter and money order for $5.50 which you
> owed me since 1931.
> Honesty is certainly the best policy to follow, and if Father Divine has
> convinced so many people to pay all their debts and to right all the wrong
> they have done, he surely must be a man of God, and a good one too.
> I will be pleased to read Father Divine's message. I have read about
> Him in the papers, but never before met one of his followers.
> I can see now why so many people believe in him, and why so many
> bad ones have turned good.
> Thank you for sending me the money and you can tell Father Divine
> for me that in causing people to do *right* always, he has indeed accomplished
> a very great good.[17]

Typical of a thousand others is this letter from Father Divine to Mr. Foster of
Asheville, North Carolina:

PEACE

April 12, 1938, *A.D.F.D.*

My dear Mr. Foster:

I write as I wish to advise receipt of yours of the 4th, in which you have informed ME that one of MY followers Miss Rebecca Love, has liquidated her debt of $100.00, balance due on a $203.00 debt. I AM indeed grateful to know of the same.

In advancing and promulgating this Standard of Righteousness, Justice and Truth in the lives and affairs of men, I AM bringing about better living conditions among them. I AM lifting a Criterion of Truth for all mankind, that the serpents of prejudice, hatred, jealousy and strife might be completely eradicated from the earth.

When men shall realize that there can never be any victory, and Peace, happiness or prosperity in wars, segregation, race prejudice, class discrimination and other negative qualities of expression, then shall be an end of depressions, wars, cosmic disasters and other destructions of life, liberty and Peace.

Despite present-day conditions, the Spirit of Righteousness is Marching on. Its work is mightier than the sword, for it is conquering the will of men, of which it is written: "Greater is he who conquers his will than he who taketh a city."

Hence, as I rise in the Spirit of MY Mind and the Mind of My Spirit within the hearts and minds of the children of men, I AM causing them to subjugate themselves unto Righteousness, Justice and Truth. Thru the Light of the same they realize there is no glory in war, for the glory of war is death, destruction, waste and depressions. But in the Light of Righteousness, with lives consecrated to the Truth, millions today are finding Peace, joy and happiness. They are mentally and Spiritually rising above the planes of mortality, losing sight of old conditions of life, as thru the reality of this Spiritual awakening, I AM manifestly establishing the Kingdom of Heaven on earth and in the lives and affairs of mankind.[18]

In a long letter to the Director of Internal Revenue, Silvio Spagnolo, who worked as a maintenance man for the Philadelphia church properties, wrote:

... during the year 1923, 24, 25 ... I maliciously avoided ... the income tax ... having been converted by God Almighty, Father Divine, I also confess having been engaged in bootlegging for a short time, and I want to ask our Government for forgiveness.

I herein enclose U.S. money orders of $500 for income tax and accumulated interest, plus $500 as an act of reparation, for having violated the law by bootlegging.

... I would appreciate it if you'd notify the Rev. M. J. Divine about it, as all the credit, all the honor goes to HIM.[19]

Constant repetition of this kind of statement has been an impressive testimony confirming Father Divine's powers to his followers.

Rejecting insurance, social security coverage, and public assistance were all considered absolutely essential as a demonstration of faith in God, Father Divine. If God is the source of all security, of eternal life, he reasoned, there is no need, among the truly saved, for economic plans that suggest even the possibility of age, illness, or death.

Several losses by fire that the Movement experienced in the thirties were interpreted as examples of persecution by enemies, with no insurance involved. Recovery from these disasters through purchase of still more properties added weight to the belief that Father Divine could overcome the world.

A selective process resulted from the economic ideology: an apprentice follower who could not see the "mystery" (substitute *charisma*) of the salvation of honest work and orderly living could never become a true follower or live in the kingdom of Father Divine.

VII

The Organization of the Peace Mission Movement

In a charismatic movement there is at first no formal organization; frequent face-to-face contacts with the leader suffice to conduct group activities. As they develop faith in his abilities members voluntarily accept his leadership and follow his suggestions or commands. Separation from him and his followers is the penalty for disregarding these rules. In this respect Father Divine's leadership in the Sayville years was the prototype of pure charisma; in order to interact with him, one had to be accepted by him as a guest in his home. Anyone who wished to be fully accepted by Father Divine must follow the "evangelical life" he taught. Only then could the supernatural powers he represented exert themselves.

Father appeared on the American scene as the head of a small family. He had already delegated responsibility for certain household duties to his wife. Guests lived with them and shared the work around the house. Other guests came for a short visit—a weekend or perhaps longer. Still others came for an interview with Father Divine and stayed for a meal. This appeared to be an example of a legal or traditional group, organized under the laws and traditions of any American family. The husband's dominance and the wife's duties and acceptance of helpful guests in a childless home is not an unusual social occurrence in America.

What was unusual about this family, what went beyond the accepted laws and mores, was the concept of Fatherhood ascribed to Major Jealous Divine by his wife and guests and the worshipful behavior his presence evoked.

In recalling his transitional phase toward becoming a charismatic figure, Father Divine would speak of having withdrawn from public preaching to avoid conflict with religious groups, his failure to interest followers in reading books, and his final conviction that those who came to him wanted the message of God from *him* directly. He had also accepted the economic function of finding work for those who needed it. As more and more people turned to Father Divine for spiritual and material aid, a more complex, formal organization than a single family, less intimate than the face-to-face meals in Divine's home, was ready to evolve. Diffusion of responsibilities among a larger number of persons was necessary.

Once Father had discovered his personal charisma attested to by others' enthusiasm for his presence, his words, or the "consciousness of his presence," he also discovered that individuals felt rewarded if they were allowed to be identified with him, be near him, and submit to his authority.

Over and over again through the years he told his followers: "You like to be with me, you like to follow me as an example, you like to serve me; and when you do you are rewarded with good health, happiness, and prosperity, If I cannot reach your needs go somewhere else." There was a continuous weeding out of those who would not voluntarily submit to the norms of the leader. Those remaining were totally committed.

Weber observed that the group around a charismatic leader not only recognizes his authority but accepts the duty of giving him complete personal devotion in order to cope with despair and express hope. Father Divine never ceased to remind his followers of the despair from which he had rescued them.

With the rush of publicity attendant on his trial, demands on Father Divine and his small family were greatly increased. Letters and requests for copies of his messages had to be answered; appeals to speak at large gatherings needed response. In return for the privilege of living in his presence and taking down his words, typing his letters, helping in the publication of various media, there developed the important role of the Secretary. It was an honorable position filled only at the personal invitation of Father Divine. Only Mother's position held more prestige, for the Secretary spent most of his or her time either with Father or in his service.

At least two male Executive Secretaries served in various capacities at various times. Well-educated members of the majority group in American society, they acted as hosts to the many visitors, screened those who sought interviews, and corresponded with newspapers and magazines. The female Secretaries were and are an integrated group of better-than-average education. There may have been as many as twenty-five at one time and fewer at other times. They served when and as long as Father wished them to. Certain Secretaries became responsible for overseeing the care of properties, others for coordinating transportation, still others for the records and typing. Thus were responsibilities diffused, but still under the continuous supervision and command of the charismatic leader. No one but Father could speak for him and one could be in his presence only at his sufferance. There was no formal plan of organization, no job description, no payroll, and no specific tenure. The Secretaries continued to serve, with their specific duties in 1978, as they did in the 1940s.

Father did not plan ahead; he moved, as he said, "volitionally." This eventually necessitated having a chauffeur with a car always ready, and several Secretaries, also with cars, in an entourage which through the years took on a cook, Father's private waitress, and Mother Divine. It was always considered an honor and a privilege to play any part in this operation. Now the movements of Mother Divine are accomplished with similar efficiency, and with many of the staff still in their original roles.

From this charismatic family of the 1930s there has evolved a maze of other groups collectively called the Peace Mission Movement, actually tied together only by their loyalty to the words of Father Divine. Among these groups are several legally incorporated churches and innumerable small businesses each identifying itself in some way with Father Divine.

The transition from the one expanding group living with Father Divine to many separated groups and individuals measuring up to his norms (even though many had never seen him) came about in an unpremeditated sequence of events.

As an aftermath of the unpleasantness at Sayville, his imprisonment, and the publicity, Father Divine became a symbol not only of salvation to his followers but of a broader struggle for religious freedom and civil rights. A well-known Harlem lawyer had defended him, Harlem papers had followed the trial, and Harlem followers were anxious to entertain and worship with him in Harlem.

In his last appearance before he went to prison he had claimed that his imprisonment was part of his plan to bring God and Heaven into this world and that great happening lay ahead for all who were with him.

Weber identifies charisma with enthusiasm; in some places he says that it is "born of enthusiasm." The dictionary equates enthusiasm with divine inspiration or possession, ecstasy, transport, ardent zeal, and fervor. All these terms and more are needed to describe the scene at Rockland Palace in Harlem in 1932 when Father Divine was released from prison. From nine in the morning until late at night Father issued challenges to the world while listeners sang, danced, and swooned:

> I came to establish the Kingdom of God in the hearts and minds of men. I
> am no race, no creed, no color, and I will not tolerate the thought of them. I
> have called unto you from every tribe and every people, every denomination, every race, every creed, every color.[1]

At the time of so-called depression, at the time of so-called limitations, at the time of so-called adverse conditions as they are supposed to be existing in the world at large, God had come out on the scene to express Himself as the master of the conditions and circumstances and as the controller of it and them. Therefore you can rejoice and I can be glad for the limitless blessings that we have, and what I have is free for one and it is free for all so long as you will accept of the Lord, and recognize your God.[2]

And when I want food, it is there too, I just don't have to take any thoughts about it—but I have come to give you something that is more than food or drink. It is more than love of food, for I have the victory over every adverse condition, whether it be physical, mental, social, financial or political; or any position in life that is in a chaotic condition, and if you desire to have the victory over it live in conformity to the life and teaching of Christ as recorded by Matthew, Mark, Luke and John according to my prerehearsed instructions and you will be abundantly blessed and freed from all undesirable conditions no matter what they may be. . . . You will no longer be segregated, or in other undesirable conditions or expressions of life, for God will be in you as He is here and will be the Master of circumstances and conditions and causes and effects.[3]

[To those who are negative to this Gospel] there will be all sorts of disasters, disappointments, accidents, and the Cosmic Forces of Nature will work contrary to them. . . . I have won in every account of all the Courts that have endeavored to prosecute my activities, my spirit, and my mission . . . and nothing has power to prohibit Me from going into any of the cities or counties . . . any state or country I wish to.[4]

To those who questioned Father Divine's mission because some claimed he was born or married in 1882, the challenger answered:

I know God did not have a beginning and he has no ending. Where did man get his wisdom before God was born? Before 1882 where was the earth? It is wonderful. If God just began—if he was born in 1882, then where were you? The Spirit of My Presence and the Presence of My Spirit is functioning with or without a Bodily Form and I have not come to bear witness or record of matter nor materiality. Learn the Mystery of God's Presence . . . relax all your preconceived ideas and opinions with all the theories and doctrines of men . . . and the very Spirit of God's Presence will be with you, with or without a person.

I say I am in ten million souls, it is wonderful, and ten million are in Me and I can live in them and have the victory over All sin and over all crime. For this cause I got in them and transformed their minds and made them willing to walk in the footsteps of Mine and recognize their Lord and their King and accept of this Principle as the only fundamental, and elect as the Lord and yet as the King to reign over them.[6]

In the presence of enthusiastic crowds and at the head of a table of participants in a communal banquet many individuals did "relax all preconceived ideas and opinions" and feel that if they but followed the mind of Father they would escape all adversity, sin, and chaos. They offered him their services when he said he wanted their love and their lives.

The next step in organization from the small family-centered group at Sayville was an informal group pooling its resources to hire a hall where Father could speak. Few churches were large enough and most ministers, as Father had predicted, were hostile to him. It was soon discovered that the Communion Banquet produced an ecstasy and a unity that went beyond the scope of a large gathering in the usual auditorium. A reporter for the Harlem paper which was most receptive to Father Divine wrote in March 1934:

> Banquet Tables, Banquet Tables, Banquet Tables, spreading throughout the world. Wherever the name of Father Divine is heard, there a banquet table can be expected, flowing with the abundance of the Promised Land, for the Great Duplicator is here, and the Holy Table that originated in Sayville, Long Island, has been duplicated many times over, in all parts of the world.

> The latest word seems to be that it has reached the Island of New Zealand on the way to the South Pole, and Songs of Praise from Merry hearts are no doubt going forth from there at this very moment, to join the great broadcast of praise. . . .

> As many, and as beautiful as they may be, however, there is none quite like the Table at which Father is present Personally, where the beauty of holiness reigns supreme, and the ugliness of mortality does not show its head in His shining presence, where only shouts of Joy, and glad songs of praise arise, and shafts of Holy Love fall from His Allseeing Eyes.[7]

Such were the emotions and convictions evoked for the follower at the Communion Banquet.

Vicarious participation in the banquet was secured by packing every empty space with onlookers, and piping the sound to every room in the building. Since the certainty or the time of Father's arrival was not known in advance, crowds sometimes formed hours before his arrival. If he did not come, followers anxious not to miss his next appearance would either return or go elsewhere seeking another possible Communion Table. During the wait the chanting of songs all directed to Father and his works contributed to the sense of unity and polarized all thought and emotions on him. Typical of these spontaneous songs was the one being repeated hundreds of times on the evening of November 29, 1934, before Father appeared at 9:30:

> See that I love you more,
> See that I love you more,
> My sweet, loving father,
> See that I love you more.

(At times the words were changed to: "See that I serve you more," and "See that I praise you more.")

Accumulating purchased or rented properties was an essential next step. Space was needed in which to hold praise services, Communions, and personal interviews with Father Divine. The property in Sayville was sold to some of the followers who continue to maintain it as a home and shrine. Father and Mother became guests of any follower or church whose invitation they felt moved to accept. No property remained in their names, but followers asked permission to give their businesses names that would identify them with Father; he granted this to any who met his standards of morality. They must sell for less than competitors, buy and sell for cash, and live an evangelical life.

Father had no title in any of the properties nor any legal responsibility for them, but when his followers furnished overnight lodging or food or services they became subject to the state and local mercantile and housing laws. The successful overcoming of these difficulties, sometimes with the help of legal advice, would often be ascribed to the charisma of the Father.

The evangelical life enjoined upon the true follower involved celibacy, even for the married. In later years Father Divine required that any married person be accepted into full participation in the Movement only after having made all legal arrangements for obligations to spouse or children. But in the early years the enthusiasm of an individual had sometimes led to difficulties with the courts. Charismatic authority found itself challenged by legal authority. The followers saw victories for Father in these cases.

The editors of one of the Movement's newspapers printed a long legal dialogue in one such case:[8]

Domestic Relations Court, Childrens' Court, County of Manhattan in the matter of Hattie Isaacs, Docket No. 502, March 1, 1935. Before Hon. Jacob Panken, Justice.

Appearances: Child Hattie Isaacs, Rebecca Isaacs, Rev. Major J. Divine, Arthur A. Madison, Esq. for Mr. Divine.

The Court: I have asked you to come here, Mr. Divine, because of what has been told me by the Mother of Hattie Isaacs. She told me that she had turned over this child, Hattie, who is now fourteen years old, to a Miss Penny. We find that this child had absented herself from Miss Penny's home, stayed away from there for eight days and nights. She said she was with somebody and somebody else. She went to moving picture shows, or went to meetings. When I asked Mrs. Isaacs why she doesn't look after the child she told me that she was living somewhere on 63rd Street. When I asked her whether she didn't feel responsible for the child, if she was not the mother of the child, she said she was not the mother of the child; that the mother of this child was God, and that God was Father Divine, and that Father Divine was in her, and that she feels no responsibility for this child. She told me that was his teaching she received. I am not interested in the mother, I am not interested in you, but I am interested in this child. She is in my charge. She is my obligation. She is my responsibility. The State has placed on me the duty and the obligation to see that this child shall have her rights, her chance; that she is to be taken care of properly; that she is to be looked after. And she has been neglected by her mother pursuant to a teaching, to a preachment which you have delivered. Everyone of us has the right to believe in his God. Some of us even say to others that we are God, but we deal with people of that kind when they become a menace to the community. It isn't normal. It isn't sane for anyone to arrogate to himself the powers which are those of the Infinite and the Supreme. And it isn't moral; it isn't proper, and it isn't right for any man to separate the natural guardians and the natural dependents. I didn't believe the woman when she told me that you preached that. I didn't think any man would preach such a doctrine. I want this mother to take her child back. I want you to tell her that you are not God, and there is no such preachment by you that you are God, otherwise I shall have to commit her for observation so that there is an inquiry as to her sanity, and determine whether the child is to be returned to the mother or sent elsewhere. I want to hear from you on that, Mr. Divine.

(Mr. Madison found it difficult to get the Judge to allow him to make an appeal that the questions asked Reverend Major J. Divine pertained to the case and nothing else. After some argument the court granted this.)

Reverend Major J. Divine, being duly sworn, testified as follows:

Q. What is your name?   A. Major J. Divine.   Q. Where do you live, sir?
A. 20 West 115th Street.   Q. Did you know Hattie Isaacs, this child before
me?   A. I do not, by name.   Q. Do you know her by appearance?   A. I
think I have seen her from time to time in the public meetings.   Q. Do you
know Rebecca Isaacs?   A. Only by sight, not by name.   Q. Rebecca Isaacs
tells me that you are God, and that as God, you are in her, and as God, as she
has been taught by you . . . she is not the mother of this child, and she told
me that is . . . the religion you teach.

(Once again Mr. Madison objected that the question was improper and was over-
ruled.)

Q. So you hold yourself out to be God to all of these people? Do you hold
yourself out to be God?

A. I preach the Gospel of Jesus Christ.

Q. Excuse me. Will you answer the question? Do you hold yourself out to be
God? Yes or No.

Mr. M. He doesn't have to answer yes or no.

The Court: Prepare a citation for contempt of Court by this counsel.

(Once again the Judge and Mr. Madison have an angry interchange, and the Judge
returns to questioning the witness.)

Q. Do you preach to these people that you are God? Did you preach to this
woman that you are God?   A. Judge, your Honor, I preach that God dwells
in every man.   Q. Did you preach to this woman that you are God?

A. I preach—

Mr. M. The question has already been answered.

Q. Do you preach—

A. I preach God in every man, not confined to one man.

Q. Do you tell me that you preach to this woman, who is the mother of this
child, that you are God?

A. I preach the gospel of Jesus, and that God dwells in every man.

Q. Is that the best answer you can make?

A. Best I can make.

Q. I'll put it this way. Do you say you are God?

(Mr. Madison objected again that such a question was not the Court's business and was rebuked and threatened with citation for contempt of court, and the judge resumed the questioning.)

Q. Do you say you are God? That will be answered yes or no, if you please. Don't evade, please. I am interested in this child.

(Mr. Madison objected and was ignored again.)

Q. Will you please, Mr. Divine?

(Mr. Madison continued to intercede and was told by the Court to step aside.)

Q. You are an intelligent man, and I believe I am. Tell me, just tell me, do you say you are God?

A. I don't have to say I am God, and I don't have to say I am not God.

Q. Well, do you say you are God?

A. I don't say either one. I said there are thousands of people call me God— millions of them, and there are millions that call me the devil, and I don't say I'm God, and I don't say I am the devil, but I produce God and shake the earth with it.

Mrs. Isaacs: Thank you, Father, God.

The Court: This woman is undoubtedly— do you see what you are doing to this woman?

A. [continuing] I do not say that I am God, and I do not say that I am the devil, but I will bring God to the consciousness of people, and I'll command man to deal justly with people, or else I'll move them out of office.

Mrs. Isaacs: Thank you, Father.

Q. Who?

A. Every Judge and ruler who will not deal justly with the people.

Q. Now this lady told me that you took her from her child, or you advised her to go live in the Community House, and so she abandoned her child. Do you advise these women to leave their homes and go to live in communities?

A. I do not, your Honor.

Q. All right, that's a direct answer. Of that I am glad. I see that you can make a direct answer.

A. But in certain circumstances—things that concern you and the Court.

Q. All right. Do you approve of this woman leaving her child?

A. I do not, your Honor.

Q. Do you direct this woman to go back to live with her child?

A. I do, if she so will to.

Q. In other words, you believe that you have the right to direct these disciples of yours?

A. I believe that I have the right for them to be governed by their highest intuition and believe that I am God, if they wish to.

Q. Do you tell them that you are God?

A. I do not tell them that I am God.

Court: That's an answer.

A. [continuing] And I don't tell them that I'm the devil, but I hear many say I'm the devil, and millions say I am God, but I'll prove to the world that God rules in the affairs of men, and none can hinder Him.

Q. What do you say about that, Mrs. Isaacs?

Mr. M.: Please don't embarrass the sister.

Q. Do you represent her too?

Mr. M.: I withdraw, I retract the question.

Q. What do you say about it, taking your child back and making a home for her, Mrs. Isaacs? You look at me. What do you say about taking the child back and making a home for her?

Mrs. I.: I say this—

Q. Do you want to make a home for this child?

Mrs.: You want me to answer that question?

Q. Yes.

Mrs. I.: I answer the question according to this. For nine years I am supporting this child, seeing she is placed, has something to eat and taking care of her the best God would have me do, which was my right by God, according to the laws, teachings and rules, and I advised the child to do the same. If the child obeys me as God teaches me and I teach her and keep to these rules and laws according to God's teachings, then I would go to the last limit of my length that he allows me to go.

Q. Who allows you to go?

Mrs. I.: Father Divine is God Almighty to me, whether he is to you or not, and this I'm willing to do my part, and if she don't, I don't care to have anything to do with her.

Q. You don't care to have anything to do with her.

Mr. M.: She said, unless she obeys.

The Court: Take this man out, will you please, officer? Show Mr. Madison a seat back there. [Addressing Mrs. I. . . .]

Q. So far as you're concerned, Divine is God?

Mrs. I.: To me he is, yes.

Court: All right. Let a commitment be made. Prepare a commitment for observation as to her sanity.

Major Divine: Judge, your Honor, may I have a word?

The Court: Yes, you may have a word.

M.D.: I would just like to say in reference to my teachings, that I would be delighted to have you, your Honor, to come to some of our public meetings.

The Court: I will.

M.D.: I would be delighted.

C.: I will, you can rest assured I will. I've got loads of children who are being abandoned by their mothers. I am going to go.

M.D.: I would be delighted to have you.

C.: Thank you very much. You can step down. What is to be done as far as the child now?

(After some conferences with the mother and social workers the child was to have a mental and physical examination because she also would not deny that Father Divine was God.)

The last interchange between the Judge and Mrs. I. was as follows:

C.: I'm going to send you to Bellevue Hospital, Mrs. Isaacs.

Mrs. I.: Thank you, Father.

C.: I think we ought to find out if you are entirely sane. What you did before me this morning wasn't the act of a sane person. You went into convulsions . . . acknowledging a witness named Divine, who was on the stand, as God Almighty. Is that right?

Mrs. I.: That's right. Thank you Father. Father Divine is right there, too. Anywhere you send me, Father Divine is right there, and ninety-nine years from today, it will be the same thing. Father Divine is God. Yes that's who he is, that's my teaching and I'm living by it.

C.: Send her to Bellevue Hospital.

(The Judge finally decided not to hold Mr. Madison in contempt of court.)

It is not clear what happened to Mrs. Isaacs and her daughter at this point but the literature of similar cases leads one to conclude that they were soon released from custody and returned to participation in the activities of Father Divine.

Where charismatic leadership coexists with legal domination, where the follow-ers of a supernatural leader are also the subjects of a political organization, mis-understandings and conflict are apt to occur. For the follower in his earlier en-thusiasm and the leader in his devotion to his mission may willfully or unknow-ingly challenge the laws of the state. Such was the case of Mrs. Isaacs. Even faced with the power of the organized state, she held to what she believed was the will of Father Divine. He in turn informed the court that she must follow her own convictions.

At this trial Father Divine's followers felt he had proved his charismatic leader-ship in triumph over legal domination. To the judge's endeavors to have him either affirm or deny his divinity, Father Divine would only reply, "I don't say I am God; and I don't say I'm the devil, but I produce God and shake the earth with it. . . . I will bring God to the consciousness of the people, and I'll command man to deal justly with the people, or else I'll move them out of office . . . every Judge and ruler who will not deal justly with the people."

To survive in a larger society a new group must search for congruence between its norms and those of the dominant groups. Hence in the 1940s various groups of followers incorporated as independent and self-governing religious bodies under Article 10 of the Religious Corporations Law of the State of New York. Such was the inception of the Movement churches which now have affiliates in Philadel-phia, New York City, Jersey City, Newark, Chicago, Washington, D.C., Miami, Tarrytown and Sayville, N.Y., Canada, Australia, Switzerland, British Guiana, the Canal Zone, West Germany, and other places. The names of these corpora-tions are the Circle Mission Church, Home and Training School, Inc., of New York; the Unity Mission Church, Home and Training School, Inc., of New York; the Nazareth Mission Church, Home and Training School, Inc., of New York; Peace Center Church and Home, Inc., of New Jersey; Palace Mission Church and Home, Inc., of New Jersey.

Among the norms established through the "Church Discipline, Constitution, and By-Laws" of these churches are these standards of responsibility for church members:

> An American flag of suitable size shall be properly displayed in the church auditorium at all times.

> We believe in a democratic form of government according to the United States Constitution and its Amendments, which grant every citizen his re-

ligious freedom and freedom of speech so long as he does not infringe on nor abridge the rights of others.

Even though as a Church we are unalterably opposed to war and the use of violence according to the Sixth Commandment, "Thou shalt not kill," we must allow the individual to take his own stand. If he is ready to let God fight his battle and has forever "laid down his shield" he would be justified in refusing any kind of military service, and under the Constitution of the United States he should be upheld in such conduct. But if he has not "reached that place in consciousness," he should take a stand according to his highest intuition and individual conviction.

We uphold the Constitution of the United States and the Declaration of Independence and believe them to be Divinely inspired.

Members and other interested persons could participate voluntarily, independently, and without compensation in providing facilities for followers, if certain Church officers approved, and if they did not have other obligations.

Other rules or norms were laid down in this formal statement of the incorporated churches, but these in particular assured that a member would not find himself at odds with the legal demands of his American citizenship. They illustrate how far the original charismatic group had moved toward organization as well as individual dependence on the spoken word of Father Divine. Father Divine maintained his control because all statements in the Discipline were documented by his utterances, and all final approval for offices of the churches was vested in him or Mother Divine.

With the appearance of the incorporated churches in the 1940s new and formal statuses were created. Each church could have an assistant pastor, appointed by Father Divine and serving at his will without pay, who is designated as Founder, Bishop and Pastor of the Peace Mission Movement. A board of trustees of nine members was to be elected at yearly corporate meetings, one-third to remain in office one year, one-third for two years and one-third for three years, thus allowing for one-third to be replaced each year. A president was to be elected for one year at the annual meeting of the church. He might or might not be a member of the board of trustees. A secretary (also designated clerk of the church) and treasurer were to be elected by the board of trustees from among their number, or they might choose the president for one of these offices. A trustee might serve any number of consecutive terms. No president could ever be elected without the approval of Father or Mother Divine, who had the right to comment on every candidate before a name was placed before the meeting.

In practice, therefore, all elected officers had the prior approval of Father or Mother Divine. This arrangement formalized and institutionalized his charisma.

The By-Laws also established a legal definition for the source and the ownership of funds used by members of the religious group. With responsibility for the contributions limited to individuals identifying themselves as members of the incorporated church, and responsibility for their use assigned to duly elected officers, Father Divine was effectively protected from legal actions involving group finances.

That such protection could have practical value for Father Divine is evident from the legal difficulties which plagued him between 1934 and 1942—all concerning property. The first of these concerned a bus used to transport followers and registered in the name of John Lamb, Executive Secretary to Father Divine. An accident involving a private car resulted in a judgment of $7,245 against John Lamb, Father Divine, and another follower. In a series of legal confrontations Father was accused of accepting and spending his followers' money. Affidavits were obtained from ex-followers to support this. In turn, Father Divine's lawyers presented 100 pages of argument and affidavits from followers indicating that Major J. Divine owed nothing and that each follower spent his own money as he saw fit. But it was not denied that Father Divine was consulted in making such decisions.

Certain affidavits support Father Divine's version of his finances at this time. His first move into a property owned by a follower is described by Charles Calloway:

> In the fall of 1931 I became interested in Father Divine and went to his home in . . . Sayville where I participated in the meetings there on a number of occasions. I became deeply interested when I learned the wonderful works of Father Divine. I heard many tell of how he fed, clothed and sheltered them when they were destitute, and hundreds healed, all without money and without price.
>
> As time passed I became more interested and felt that I wanted to help in this work if possible, as Father was the only one I had found who was working for purely an unselfish purpose, and accepting nothing for his services.
>
> I was independent financially, having retired from active work on the railroads in 1927, and I offered Father a sum of money to be turned over to anyone he might suggest to help carry out his work. This he refused saying that he never solicited or accepted gifts or contributions in any form and had no connection with anyone who did, for his work was absolutely independent, and he told me to use the money for whatsoever I would desire to see him use it for and he would be satisfied.

For more than ten years I had a number of apartments under lease on 135th Street . . . in one of which I made my home. In the late fall of 1931 and the winter of 1932, Father Divine was in such demand at public meetings where he had been invited to speak, that he was making the trip from Sayville to New York City almost daily, and still desiring to be of service, I invited him and his immediate family and guests to come and live in my home.

This invitation was accepted about March, 1932, and for about eight months my home became known as Father Divine's New York Headquarters, and was often referred to as the Peace Mission, a term that was rapidly growing in use among the followers. In the late fall of 1932, one Lena Brinson, who also had a home to which she had frequently invited Father Divine, leased a building at 20 West 115th Street. This building she used for meeting rooms, restaurants and dormitories where she sold the meals for ten to fifteen cents and sleeping accommodations for two dollars a week. She came to my home several times and requested Father Divine to come and speak at some of her meetings, and I believe he did two or three times during the following three months. She also repeatedly invited Father Divine to be her guest, and urged me on several occasions to allow her to share in the privilege of having him in her home personally.

In November of 1933, after many urgent requests on her part, Father Divine agreed to go and she placed at his personal disposal an office and an apartment on the top floor of the building. It was agreed that Mrs. Calloway and I should close our home and cooperate with Mrs. Brinson in maintaining the 115th Street home where there was room for all of us.

In this way the 20 West 115th Street address became generally known as Father Divine's Peace Mission Headquarters, and people were attracted there from all over the world because of Father's presence, but there is no organization, association, or organized group known as the Peace Mission Movement. Those who gather there do so voluntarily, there is no list of names and addresses, and they are absolutely unidentified. They pay no fees, make no donations, undertake no responsibilities, and there are no collections taken at any time. Father Divine does not participate in the financing of the place, neither does he or has he ever received any returns from it. It is not connected with any other place known as Father Divine's Peace Mission, and there is no group of individuals back of it, other than those who voluntarily devote their time and services cooperatively in the operation of it. In fact, the term Father Divine's Peace Mission has no reference to any organized group, but refers rather to the mission and purpose of Father Divine on earth, as the apostrophe "s" signifies, rather than anything else.

All of the meeting places, homes or businesses under the term Father Divine's Peace Mission . . . are conducted in the same way. They are the personal homes or businesses or independent cooperative enterprises of Father Divine's followers who live and work in them. They have no connection with Father Divine personally, although it is true those who maintain them seek his advice and cooperation as the recognized spiritual head of all those who are concerned.[9]

Eddie O. Littlejohn presented to the Supreme Court of New York County an account of his participation in various business activities and his practice of the way of life taught by Father Divine. He swore that he "believes one hundred percent in principles advocated by Father Divine, and has been a believer and follower for a period of more than five years."[10]

In 1932 or 1933, Littlejohn and several friends conducted a meeting place and restaurant serving Father Divine's followers at Laurel Garden on East 116th Street between Madison and Park Avenues. Father Divine visited there to speak as a guest on several occasions, but had nothing to do with the finances. Mr. Littlejohn operated meeting rooms and restaurants at two other locations as well as three apartments which were known as Father Divine's Peace Mission Rooming House and Dining Room. Father Divine did not participate in their operation, but his principles were followed. The sexes were segregated, room rent was set at a dollar and a quarter a week, and meals were sold for not more than ten or fifteen cents. Finally, Mr. Littlejohn and other followers opened a coal business which sold coal at less than the going price to other followers.

Despite these and many other affidavits in support of Father Divine, it was apparent that the court doubted assertions that Father Divine did not have access to funds. He denied that he did, his lawyer denied it, and his followers, to whom this was another example of prejudice and discrimination, supported him. It was finally agreed between the lawyers that the judgment against John Lamb would be honored, and the case was dropped.

The *Spoken Word* printed page after page of affidavits to establish the independence of the followers and Father Divine's unwillingness to accept cash from them. In the minds of the followers, this case was another victory for him over unjust courts.

The most protracted litigation centered on Thomas Brown and his wife Verinda, who convinced the court that during the years between 1930 and 1937 they had given over $4,000 to Father Divine. While loyal followers supported Father Divine, from 1937 to 1942 three different courts directed Father Divine to repay the money. Father maintained that he did not accept money for his spiritual services. If indeed money was involved he held that the Browns had voluntarily spent it for material services rendered. The *Spoken Word* described this as an attempt to rob the followers. Father Divine refused to accept the legality of the judgment and moved to Philadelphia. The followers looked upon this move as another triumph. He described it as a punishment for New York City where he had taken thousands off the relief rolls and converted many from their criminal ways.

With the creation of the legally incorporated churches after 1941, it was clearly stated in the By-Laws[11] that all contributions must come voluntarily from members only and become the responsibility of the president and board of trustees, with the advice and counsel of Father Divine. The board was to be responsible for all church business and material affairs, under the supervision of the president, including ownership of church property, leasing of church premises, and maintenance. The president would have two votes on any matter before the board.

No public gifts or contributions would be accepted except for services rendered for food or lodging. Neither Father Divine, his assistant pastor, nor any officers were to receive compensation.

With some modification in the number of officers this remains today the formal structure of the church. The president of each church has great moral as well as formal power since he has direct responsibility to Father or Mother Divine. A number of officers can be held legally responsible for the funds of the membership. All transactions are still in cash, and the funds of each church apparently are invested in real property in which members live, as well as worship.

No details of income or expenditure are given in the treasurer's report at the annual church meeting for business and election of officers. A typical treasurer's report is devoted primarily to praise of Father Divine. Such a report was submitted by the treasurer of the Nazareth Mission Church of Drummoyne, Australia, for 1967:[12]

> Thank You Father and Mother for Your Beautiful Ever Presence that gives us Peace, Love and Unity and the desire to love and serve You. In this Church and Training School where we are taught by our Bishop and Pastor in an atmosphere of cleanliness and Virtue, free from mortality's versions, there is abundance for the minds and bodies of all who come. As You said Father, "All who enter harmoniously will be blessed." So may it be Father Dear.

> Visitors are given *New Days* to read that they may take Your Words away with them to read and re-read. We thank You for all who have been able to rest awhile and be re-newed in the Peace, Love and Purity which the Consciousness of Your Presence brings.

The Church is maintained in good order, repairs being done as necessary. The garden is a joy, showing how You have taken the curse out of the ground, and it is bringing forth its abundance for Your Holy Communion Table.

All work is done with joy in loving co-operation and sweet Unity to the Glory of Your Holy Name, knowing it is the Father alone Who doest all things.

Thank You Father and Mother Dear, we appreciate being a member and being allowed to work in Father's Vineyard, ever over-coming self, by continual praise and devotion to our Father-Mother God.

Father is our Source of supply and He blesses us abundantly. All our accounts are paid as they come due, and we are happy to say we owe no man. All the glory and praise go to our one Eternal Father and Mother because we know You Are God.

We glorify You for all the blessings and healings poured out on all who can receive them, and we praise Your Holy Name.

It is Wonderful and a continued joy to see Your Words, "I have given a body to every worth while thing," fulfilled, as we see Honesty, Righteousness, Truth and Justice taking on more and more bodies today.

For all Your Beautiful Love and Patience, Father-Mother we humbly thank You.

Respectfully submitted,
Treasurer

The By-Laws direct that a list of contributions made by members for such special purposes as purchase or maintenance of property be kept for business reasons. All purchases and payments of any kind must be in cash on delivery and bear the endorsement of the president or other officers. But:

We do not take thought for the morrow by keeping a record of cash on hand, neither do we minimize our blessings by keeping a record of cash received and paid out. God told Abraham, "As far out in the land as you can see can be for your inheritance."

Therefore the Treasurer shall be unable to make a report on any of these things. However, at the Annual Meeting each year he shall report to the Members whether there are any unpaid bills or obligations and whether he has cash on hand to meet them, and how much. He may also give a general report of what has been done throughout the year with Church funds, and just what activities have been carried on into which financial dealings entered.

Even before incorporation of the churches followers had listed their occupations with the Peace Mission Movement, but each individual or group of individuals remained an independent entity. The businesses did not belong to an organized movement nor to the churches. But, to remain identified with the Peace Mission of Father Divine, they must observe certain practices. They should maintain low prices, buy and sell for cash, take no tips or gifts, and refrain from dealing in tobacco or liquor, as described in the section on overcoming the depression.

The result of these two forms of organization, religious and economic, with the same individuals often taking part in both a church of the Movement and an occupation identified with it, was to create a religious community and subculture in which, as Father had urged, a follower could lose his old identity and devote his full energies to the religious life and Father Divine. Although many followers still worked in the "world," they returned to sleep, study, worship, and help with the work of one of the churches, which was also their home and "training school." True followers do not need to go outside the organized activities of the church for recreation. The followers rent their own educational movies, watch selected television programs in public rooms, use their own gymnasiums, conduct their own adult education program, and create skits and dance programs as a form of worship. They eat in their own restaurants or at the Communion Table of their church. They travel from one property of the Movement to the next by the "church cars," driven by coworkers, often serviced and garaged by followers. They may spend their vacations at one of the estates or hotels of the Movement. They may invest their money in the properties of some church or business conducted by the followers.

Father Divine stressed ownership of property as a sign of spiritual success. Individuals and churches in the Movement invested in many center-city properties in several cities, as well as in property in Ulster County, New York. (Property is listed in an appendix.) All the property is used by members of the various churches for housing, business, or worship services. Since much of it was purchased for cash during the depression or immediately following the Second World War, before the rise in real estate values, it represents a real increase in the wealth of its owners. At one time it was estimated to be worth at least $10 million.

A tenet of the movement is "that all men, who are worthy to live, shall live well, with the abundance of every comfort and convenience that modern society can produce."

Just as in the 1930s followers had vied with each other to provide housing for Father Divine, so this tradition continued as the churches were incorporated. Each church and hotel furnished a suite of rooms for Father and a separate one for Mother, since they did not practice the worldly form of marriage. Each building owned by followers was also the "home" of Father Divine. Each group of followers felt that the Spirit was always with them, but they wanted the privilege of entertaining the "Body" as well.

In 1953 Father and Mother Divine were presented by one of the churches with an estate in an exclusive section of the Philadelphia suburbs. It belongs to the Palace Mission Church of New York and is called Woodmont, the Mount of the House of the Lord; it is considered the home of Mother and Father Divine. Its huge castle-like main house is surrounded by seventy-three acres of beautifully landscaped lawns and gardens. A swimming pool, tennis courts, and delightful paths through forest, lawns, and gardens frame a view of many miles of estate country. In 1968 a unique stone shrine to Father Divine was unveiled on the highest point of land in the county, beside the room in which he had his office from 1953 to 1965.

The estate immediately became a symbol of the spiritual and material success of Father Divine and his Movement. It was identified with events predicted in the Bible. In referring to it the Movement quotes Isaiah 2:2,3:

> And it shall come to pass in the last days, that the mountain of the Lord's house shall be established in the top of the mountains, and it shall be exalted above the hills; and all nations shall flow to it.

> And many people shall go and say, Come ye, and let us go up to the mountain of the Lord, to the house of the God of Jacob; and we will walk in his paths; for out of Zion shall go forth the law, and the word of the Lord from Jerusalem.

And Father Divine indicated its significance as follows:

> ... the Mount of the House of the Lord has been lifted up ... and we are the fulfillers and partakers of this great unfoldment of righteousness ... the law shall go out and they shall say: "Let us go up to the House of the Lord, that He may teach us His Ways."

A visit to Woodmont and taking Communion there are probably the most rewarding experience that a follower can have. Belonging to the staff which maintains the estate is also a great honor. A chance to serve there in any capacity is welcomed by all.

It is here that it is possible to experience the primary-group nature of the rank and file of the Movement. They have known each other for five to forty years. They have worked together, traveled together in the church cars, lived together in buildings they own jointly, and eaten together at Communions served by fellow believers and in restaurants owned and staffed by "brothers" and "sisters."

The hours spent at Woodmont are the high points of the week, partly because of the beauty and spiritual significance of the estate, but especially because of the shrine to Father Divine. Followers come to visit it from all over the world. Those close by may come every week if possible.

Any weekend will attract cars from a dozen states. Church cars begin arriving as soon as services in the Philadelphia churches are finished on Sunday, so that by one-thirty or two o'clock there are little knots of men and women standing around the gardens and sitting in the shade of huge trees, men with men and women with women. There is much small talk and polite joking as well as discussion of the good things Father did, and how he brought about the end of segregation, as illustrated by the latest news on the radio. Some men listen to transistor radios. There is no separation by race; only by sex. Light faces appear in every group, although usually in a minority.

Before 1965, the climax of a visit used to be the appearance of Father and Mother Divine, some time between two and four, usually walking out on the high porch of the mansion, or serving the Communion (a banquet) in the former chapel, a beautiful room imported many years ago from France.

During this waiting period one could listen to the informal talk of the followers, wandering from group to group, and exchange pleasant conversation. When the Communion occurred attention focused on that, with singing, testimonies, and other ceremonies. This was the most moving of all the services, with Father and Mother Divine present. Even in the absence of Father's body, followers today are still sure of his presence. Foreign guests or distinguished "strangers" are invited to speak, and the setting is one of great beauty.

Since the shrine was completed and dedicated in September 1968, followers have come from all over the world to worship there. The public is invited to visit the estate and the shrine on Sunday afternoons.

The official literature describes the shrine:

> The shrine at Woodmont, powerful in its simplicity, denotes the personal life of Father Divine. Its peaceful atmosphere conveys his serenity and humility. Its strength and purity of line, his staunch stand for the high moral and spiritual values of life made clear by his own example which are the

foundation stones of the Peace Mission Movement as it stands today, a bulwark of faith in a troubled world.

Its purpose is twofold. It is the Holy Sanctuary enshrining the body of God Father Divine and it is a reminder of the consistency and continuity of God's covenant fulfilled from the beginning of biblical history to the present time. "And the Lord shall establish Thee an Holy people unto Himself, as He has sworn unto thee, if thou shalt keep the commandments of the Lord thy God, and walk in his ways." Deuteronomy 28:9.[13]

VIII

Religious Orders of the Movement

The highest spiritual goal, for followers of Father Divine's Peace Mission Movement, is achieving the status of a Rosebud, Lily-Bud, or Crusader. From observation it appears that approximately half the active participants at meetings wear the distinctive uniforms that identify each of these three "orders." The more exclusive honor of being a Secretary is limited to from fifteen to twenty-five women, and only one man—the Executive Secretary of the Circle Mission Church.

Rosebuds wear dark red or maroon jackets with a white *V*, for virtue, over their hearts, and navy blue skirts. They and the Crusaders, who are male, conduct the Wednesday night meetings. They act as choir, and on special occasions become dramatic artists and dancers, produce playlets, and demonstrate interpretive dancing and marching formations for special functions like the Wedding Anniversary, Woodmont Anniversary, and Fourth of July celebrations. Their ages run from early childhood to middle age. No more than fifty have been assembled at one service, but Philadelphia, New York, and New Jersey churches apparently number at least a hundred in their followings. Photographs of church groups in other countries—Germany, Switzerland, Australia, the Canal Zone, and Canada —show many fewer—only one to ten younger ladies in Rosebud costume.

Crusaders are men of all ages, from young children to oldest men, who, like the Rosebuds and Lily-Buds, have expressed a desire to live up to their Creeds, Commandments, and other articles of faith. (Samples of these various declarations follow.) Like Rosebuds and Lily-Buds, too, they devote their time, energy, and whatever money they wish to contribute to the Movement, except when they work at jobs in the "world" during the day, or are doing their military service. During the Second World War some were conscientious objectors and accepted alternative civilian service.

All three groups conduct services, act as choirs, and, individually, as readers of the *New Day* or the Bible, King James Version. Many individuals participate in conducting the services; anyone may start a group song or sing a solo. Anyone may teach a new song to the worshippers merely by rising in his place and singing it until others can follow. The words of the songs are original with the Movement, but the music may be borrowed.

All the orders take vows of chastity and do not live in marital status even though they may once have been married. Men and women dwell in separate buildings or on separate floors and many have roommates of the same sex.

On formal occasions—banquets, celebrations, praise services, and Communions (which are often banquets)—Crusaders wear powder blue tuxedo coats, white shirts, black ties, and dark trousers. Some may bring (as do a few Rosebuds and Lily-Buds) musical instruments—a cornet, violin, drums, triangle, guitar, or saxophone—to meetings with them and accompany the choir, the pianist, or the organist. There is much spontaneous musical performance.

Not more than a hundred men in all were observed wearing Crusaders' costumes, and not over fifty at any one time, even at the biggest celebrations. In photographs from other countries only three men in the Canal Zone church appear in uniform.

Lily-Buds, the older women, participate in musical, reading, and testimonial ways in all of the services. In their green jackets trimmed with white they appear to be the largest contingent of uniformed followers. Perhaps 100 were observed at different times wearing this jacket, but never more than seventy-five at one time. In photographs from Switzerland, Germany, the Canal Zone, and Australia there are only two to a dozen in each church group wearing the garb of a Lily-Bud.

Although the largest proportion of people at most gatherings wear one of these uniforms, another group of perhaps forty percent do not appear so honored— usually older women, a smattering of older men, and one or two adolescent boys. Even these followers, it is believed, aspire to become Rosebuds, Lily-Buds, or Crusaders, and may be able to when their conscience assures them they can live up to the documents of the orders.

The Movement is essentially one large religious order with four divisions of followers who have vowed they will give all their love and time to Father Divine and will live, through his commandments, by the Sermon on the Mount and the Creeds of the Peace Mission Movement. Those who cannot achieve this leave the Movement and return to the larger world outside.

Secretaries have no separate creeds to follow. As a rule, they have previously been

Rosebuds. Mother Divine was originally a Rosebud and still wears the jacket and skirt on certain occasions.

The Rosebuds' Creed and Other Documents

A Rosebud's Heart

A Rosebud's heart is submissive, meek and sweet;
Is your great *Redeemer's* Throne;
Where CHRIST alone is heard to speak;
And where CHRIST alone reigns within;
Where CHRIST has been selected by them
To reign as LORD and KING;
Where every other thought of person or mankind
Has been completely dethroned for Him.

A Rosebud's heart is a heart of LOVE,
That is lost in the Will of GOD;
That will not doubt and will not fear,
But will sacrifice their all to GOD.

A Rosebud's heart is a heart that is WILLING
To suffer hardships and oppositions;
That will stand even with all the world of criticism
Being focused directly at them.

A Rosebud's heart is a heart so KIND,
That takes GOD in their minds,
And never, never, never, never
Will attempt to leave Him behind.

A Rosebud's heart is a heart so TRUE,
That will do what CHRIST says do,
And will not doubt a Word He says,
No matter what others do.

A Rosebud's heart is a heart so STRONG,
That cannot be changed by men;
That looks diligently on the LORD,
And accepts Him alone as KING.

A Rosebud's heart is a heart where CHRIST ALONE shall reign,
Since Christ in thought

And in all their minds
Has truly been enthroned.

A Rosebud's heart is a heart so TRUE
That will not murmur nor complain;
That will not doubt and will not fear,
Matters not what others think.

A Rosebud's heart is a heart that LOVES
The LORD with all they have.

A Rosebud's heart is a heart for GOD,
That is what you all should claim.
You all should have a Rosebud's heart,
That is PURE, MEEK and SWEET;
A heart as the fertile, VIRGIN ground of Salvation
Where CHRIST will take His Seat.

A Rosebud's heart it is so FINE;
'Tis LOVING, 'Tis PEACEFUL and KIND.

A Rosebud's heart is filled with JOY,
That has the LORD entwined.
In PEACE and LOVE I will abide
In the Rosebud's heart evermore;
That is, if they but will be TRUE
And do what I bid them do.

A Rosebud's heart that really is TRUE,
Is CONSECRATED to GOD;
It takes no thought what it should do,
But will follow the LORD.
It is willing to suffer hardships and pain,
It is willing to labor and toil;
BECAUSE IT IS A ROSEBUD'S HEART
IT IS THE HEART OF GOD!

Rosebuds' Pledge

FATHER DIVINE, GOD ALMIGHTY,
We Pledge our Hearts and Love to You,
Our strength to serve you,
Our minds to be focused directly upon You,

Our lips to praise YOU,
Our lives to praise you,
Our sacred Honor to acknowledge you in all our ways,
That we may be with you throughout all eternity,
One spirit, one mind and one body,
Lost and absorbed, once and forever, in your Holy Will!

Rosebuds' Ten Commandments

1. The "Sweets" shall forever obey, cherish, respect and praise their Lord and Saviour, FATHER DIVINE, above all else.

2. We shall always have a kind word and smile for others.

3. We shall keep guile from our lips.

4. We shall have one mind, one aim, and one purpose—GOD, FATHER DIVINE.

5. We shall rejoice at the blessings of others.

6. We will endeavor to let our every deed and action express virginity.

7. We will deny ourselves and consecrate our heart, mind, soul and body to the Cause.

8. We will stand by our Conviction to love GOD, even if all others oppose us.

9. We will never, no never condemn or find fault with anything our Saviour may say or do.

10. We shall at all times recognize the all-seeing Eye of our Lord and be the same, knowing that He is always in the midst of us.

Rosebudship Degree

Real True Rosebuds are at all times submissive, meek and sweet; they have hearts where Christ alone is heard to speak and where Jesus reigns alone.

These are set apart and have made themselves a living sacrifice to God; therefore at times they are called "The Sweets," whereto all True Rosebuds are required to attain. If they fail to come to this place in consciousness, and fail to express the Holiness of Jesus and the Virginity of Mary, and become to be the reproduction and repersonification of both it and them, the attributes and characteristics of Life they lived, they are not expressing a Real Rosebud's classification, neither are they Virtuous and Holy unto God. To be Real True Rosebuds you must reproduce and repersonify the very Virtues of Mary and the Holiness of Jesus, and much more is required of those who are real "Sweets."

To be True Virgins according to your real classifications, you must be Virtuous in Spirit and mind as well as in bodily form. Therefore, the bitterness of anger, resentment and jealousy would destroy all of your virginity, physically, spiritually and mentally; hence, Real True Virgins, which are Rosebuds in reality, they will not allow resentment, anger and prejudice, nor any other detestable tendency, to spoil their character. If you are corrupt mentally, spiritually and physically, the honor of your Virginity, Honesty and Virtue will be completely annihilated; for you must have a Virtuous Spirit and Mind and be untouched by the Wicked One, and absolutely undefiled to be as MY Spotless Virgin Bride, for if you are not Virtuous in spirit, heart and mind you cannot be real "Sweets."

Therefore, I hope all who are concerned and interested in a Spotless, Virtuous life, will take cognizance of "The Sweets' Endeavors" and be able to reproduce and manifest the fullest measure, all of "The Sweets' Endeavors"; for this is your calling, all True Rosebuds, whereto you are called. Therefore, abstain from all appearance of evil, refuse to anger, use obscenity, profanity or vulgarity. Serve the Lord your God with all your might and refuse to use any of your energy to fuss or fight.

Rosebuds' Endeavor

To copy after Your Ways, being not different or odd;
To prove it is truth, when we say You are God,
To live pleasing to You is our hearts' desire,
To do only the things that You would admire;
To trust You in all things and never, never doubt, but
To know we'll always be cared for and never go without;
To follow diligently as You pave the way,
To never shrink, or even take a thought to go astray;
To uphold and stand with You, Father, no matter what may come.
To let Your Thoughts be our thoughts; ye, let all be one.
To hold back not one thing, 'tho it may seem small;
To be not selfish, resentful or jealous at all;
To respect everyone, child or adult;

To never anger, never pout and never sulk.
To claim not a thing, but be willing to share.
To be not aggressive, greedy or unfair;
To say not a word for selfish justification,
To keep Holy and Divine our every conversation;
To blame not another but repent for our own faults,
To stay ever in harmony in words, deeds and thoughts;
To speak only words we would want You to hear;
To think only thoughts we would say in Your ear;
To smile only smiles pleasing to You;
To touch only the clean things as You would want us to.
To step where Your Spirit has stepped before;
To give heart, mind and body for they all are Yours,
To write not a word we want You not to see;
To breathe not a breath hidden from You in secrecy;
To take not an object, then to You would not show.
To read not a word we wouldn't want You to know.
To make over others neither admiration or fuss, but
To show appreciation only to You, for what's done for us;
To listen not to idle gossip, what others might say;
To take no thought, nor plan for the next day;
To taste not a crumb that has been hidden from Thee;
To be ever thankful for things already received;
To spend not a moment if we thought You knew not where;
To make not a motion, made if Personally You weren't there;
To love, honor and reverence You wherever we may be;
To let You bear record of our presence or our absentee;
To make every word we speak real and true;
To ask not of another, but ask only of You;
To let nothing ever break us apart;
To keep You forever, The Sweet of our hearts; and
To be by all these things, united forever
To you; this is the Sweets' sincerest endeavor!

Beatitudes of Gospel of a Real True Rosebud

Blessed is the Rosebud that cherishes her FATHER's Love above all
   else.
Blessed is the Rosebud who has and portrays momently a Rosebud's
   heart.
Blessed is the Rosebud who has naught against her fellow brother.
Blessed is the Rosebud in whose mouth is found no guile, no idle
   chatter.

Blessed is the Rosebud who expresses her virtue in her daily deeds and actions.

Blessed is the Rosebud whose mind is staid in a positive direction.

Blessed is the Rosebud who is not wasteful but is practical and profitable.

Blessed is the Rosebud who does not always have the last word.

Blessed is the Rosebud who denies herself with gladness.

Blessed is the Rosebud who is the sample and example of the teachings of Jesus Christ.

Blessed is the Rosebud whose happiness is the Body of God.

Blessed is the Rosebud who is respectable, quiet, sincere, and truthful.

Blessed is the Rosebud who walks in the statutes of True Americanism.

Blessed is the Rosebud whose "All and All" is her Beloved FATHER DIVINE.

WE THANK YOU, FATHER AND MOTHER DIVINE!

The Lily-Buds' Creeds and Other Documents Pertaining to Them

Commandments

We will live every day without speaking a critical thought of any human being.

We will always think of others and not of ourselves.

We will let these bodies be a living sacrifice continually.

We will always keep this mind of Christ in us.

We will always be desirable.

We will never be aggressive, greedy or unfair.

We will never be exalted or selfish.

We will never be a pretender but real, real, real!

We will live so Christ will be seen in every way.

We will tell God everything and never try to hide.

We will always keep GOD's Name Holy.

We will love everyone as God loves us.

We will have no division among us.

We will be courteous to everyone at all times.

We will never let anything come between our soul and our Saviour.

We will praise you continually from the depths of these hearts.

We will always be mindful how we entertain strangers.

We will co-operate in every way.

We will always exalt God above everything else.

We will keep GOD'S Commandments at all times.

We will recognize GOD'S Deity at all times.

We will not justify ourselves for any cause whatsoever.

We will keep Your Commandments, FATHER, forever.

We will always love, honor, respect and obey our Lord and Saviour
above everyone else.

Lily-Buds' Endeavor

To keep Your commandments every moment of the day;

To praise YOU continually in every way;

To live pleasing to YOU at all times;

To let Your light in us always shine;

To never doubt YOU no matter what YOU may say or do;

To know every word YOU speak is real and true;

To never get angry or resentful at any time;

To always be sweet, loving and kind;

To always stay meek and lowly down at YOUR feet;

To always remember YOU mean just what you Preach;

To stand true no matter what may come;

To always in us let Your will be done;

To love, honor and reverence YOU wherever we may be;

To stand to our religious conviction whatever the penalty may be;

To never be jealous of anyone;

To always rejoice at the blessings whenever they come;

To give our bodies a living sacrifice to YOU;

To do with them as YOU will do;

To be willing to suffer for our hearts' conviction;

To be willing to stand no matter what the accusation;

To be willing to die at any time

To hold up the name of FATHER DIVINE;

To always have a smile whether child or adult;

To prove our love for YOU in words, deeds and thoughts;

To never gossip, or backbite;

To never talk negative, fuss or fight;

To never criticize or be rude to anyone;

To always search ourselves and see what we have done;

To let YOU be first in everything;

To love and adore YOU and let Your praises ring;

To never complain or find fault anywhere;

To always be willing our blessings to share;

To live pure, holy, virtuous and clean;

To never live in races, colors or creeds;

To abstain from all human affection, fancies and pleasure;

To stay away from mortality's versions;
To deny self and all its ways;
To give God All the praise; To hold YOU in our hearts forever;
This is the Lily-Buds' Endeavor.

Lily-Buds' Consecration

We, the Lilies of the Peace Mission Movement, do this night
Consecrate and dedicate our whole lives to the Cause and
Service of Almighty GOD, FATHER DIVINE.

To honor HIM, respect, love and obey HIM;
To do everything that is pleasing to HIM in every way;
To serve whensoever and wheresoever HE Wills or Desires us to;
To always be honest, sincere, competent, faithful and true.

To keep always His Name Holy, and in greatest and highest esteem;
To keep our thoughts pure, virtuous and holy and our words the same;
To walk circumspectly before the world, so that It will see the Life of
    Christ exemplified in us,
And glorify Our Father here in Heaven on Earth.
To harmonize with HIS Ideas and Opinions;
To keep company only with His Mind and Spirit;
To carry Sunshine, gladness, peace and love everywhere;
To consecrate and dedicate every moment of the day In sweet devotion
    and adoration;
To let our consecration be a holy one;
For this is the dedication and consecration
Of heart, mind, body and soul.

Lily-Buds' Creed

To never argue, fuss, or fight;
To always remember what YOU have done for us;
To always be honest, competent and true;
To do just what YOU would have us do;
To never give anyone an ugly look, but always A Smile, for we know
    that is YOU;
To never be exalted, but always meek and sweet;
To always remember what YOU teach.
To never hate another for what they may do or say;
To never grow weary or tired of this Holy Way;
To never condemn or find fault anywhere;

To always remember You are there.
To be just like YOUR Spotless Bride;
To be pure, clean, undefiled;
To always be willing in YOUR Spirit and Mind to abide;
To always be sweet, loving and kind.
To never hold friendly conversations with the opposite sex,
Only on business, as YOU have said;
To express holiness and virtue, wherever we may be;
To live all of this with YOU we plead;
For this is the Lily-Buds' Creed.

WE THANK YOU, FATHER AND MOTHER DIVINE!

The Crusader's Creed

The Crusader's Declaration
Concerning God

1. I know deep down in my heart that FATHER DIVINE is GOD—that
   HE is the Personification of GOD in a Bodily Form.
2. I believe in and accept as Divinely inspired, the King James Version of
   the Old and the New Testaments of the Holy Bible, and I embrace it as
   my Rule Book of Life.
3. I believe that FATHER DIVINE fulfils the Scriptural Prophecy of the
   Second Coming of CHRIST for the Christian World and the Coming
   of the Messiah for the Jewish World.
4. I believe in the FATHERHOOD of GOD and in the Brotherhood of
   man.
5. I believe in the Sacred, Holy, Spiritual Marriage of FATHER DIVINE,
   Who Is our Father–Mother–God, to HIS Spotless Virgin Bride,
   MOTHER DIVINE, Who before the World was, Was Predestined
   to be, and now is the Symbol of the Church without Spot or Wrinkle.
6. I believe that the Marriage of FATHER DIVINE to MOTHER
   DIVINE was Predestined to be; that it is the Marriage of the LAMB
   and the BRIDE; and that it Symbolizes the Marriage of CHRIST to the
   Church, the Union of GOD and Man, and the Fusion of Heaven and Earth.
7. I believe that FATHER DIVINE is my Real FATHER and that
   MOTHER DIVINE is my Real MOTHER and that I never had another.
8. I believe in the Actual Ever Presence and Omni-Presence of GOD and
   also in HIS Omniscience, Omnipotence, and Omnilucence.
9. I believe that the Spirit of the Consciousness of the Presence of GOD
   is the Source of all Supply and that it always has and always will, as it
   does, Satisfy every Good Desire.

10. I believe that all things are possible with GOD and that HE will keep me in the Secret Place of the Most High if I TRUST HIM Whole-heartedly and make a Wide-Open Sacrifice.

11. I believe that I was with GOD before the World was; that I, in this physical body, will inherit Eternal Life; and that this physical body will never die if I live the Life of Christ and keep the Faith according to the Teachings of FATHER DIVINE.

12. I believe in the Life and Teachings of Jesus, the CHRIST, as recorded in the Gospels of Matthew, Mark, Luke and John and especially as set forth in Jesus' Sermon on the Mount as given in the 5th, 6th and 7th Chapters of Matthew.

Concerning Country

13. I believe that America was predestined to be the Birthplace of the Kingdom of GOD on Earth.

14. I believe in the official documents of the United States of America— the Declaration of Independence and the Constitution with its Bill of Rights and Amendments—that they were Divinely inspired and that they take their places with the Old and New Testaments of the Holy Bible as instruments of the synonymous teachings of Democracy, Brotherhood, Americanism, Christianity and True Judaism.

15. I believe in the Flag of the United States of America and hereby Pledge my Allegiance to it and to the Republic for which it stands.

16. I believe that the Symbols of the Flag of the Free—Liberty, Unity, Freedom, Equity and Justice—shall be seen in every Land, as well as "Old Glory" itself, as concrete evidence of the True Significance of the Flag of the United States of America.

Concerning Man

17. I believe that all men are created by GOD and come before HIM equal to and independent of each other in HIS Sight.

18. I believe that all men are endowed by their Maker and Creator with not only equal, but the same inalienable Rights, such as the Rights to Life, Liberty and the Reality of Happiness and such as the Freedom of Religious Worship, the Freedom of Expression, the Freedom to assemble peacefully, the Freedom from want and the Freedom from fear.

19. I believe, further, that every man has the Right to live where he chooses, work where he is qualified, attend the school of his own choice, ride on any train, bus, trolley, taxi, boat or airplane, and use any public facility; such as hotels, restaurants, depots, parks, playgrounds, gymnasiums, swimming pools, golf courses, concert halls, museums, cultural exhibits

and lectures—without respect to his so-called race, creed, color or nationality.

20. I believe that every man has the Responsibility, not only to claim and use these above mentioned Rights and Freedoms for himself, but also the Responsibility to accord these Rights and Freedoms to his fellow man and to protect his fellow man from being denied of them.

21. I believe that every man has the Responsibility to be completely independent, to support himself, to owe no man, neither to give or take gifts, tips, or bribes, or to accept anything which he has not earned nor paid for.

22. I believe that every man has as his Birth-right the Freedom and Liberty to stand alone, to live his own Life, to think, speak and act according to his own Highest Intuition and Volition, to recognize no master other than his GOD as revealed to him from within, and therefore, to be Free from all ties and bonds of personalities, including those of friends, so-called mother, father, sister, brother, so-called husband, wife, son, daughter, and other so-called kin.

Therefore, We, the Inter-National, Inter-Racial, Inter-Denominational Youth of FATHER DIVINE's Universal Peace Mission Movement:

Believe that it is our Reasonable Service to our God, to our Country, to our Church, to our fellow man and to ourselves, by living to the letter Daily Lives of Virtue, Purity, Virginity and Holiness to present our bodies as Living Sacrifices in fulfilment of our official Religious and Political Documents.

IX

Survival
and the
Problem
of
Succession

"This is God's day now!"

Mother Divine, September 10, 1965

The hour had come! It was two-thirty Friday morning, September tenth, nineteen hundred and sixty-five. The place was Woodmont, the Mount of the House of the Lord. Out of the stillness of the night came a call that summoned those closest to Father Divine Personally, His immediate staff to His side. Mother Divine was already there. Our Beloved Lord and Savior Father Divine had seen fitting and necessary to throw off the Precious Holy Little Body that millions all over the world love and adore more than life itself. It was now their holy pleasure, as Followers of the Lamb, to rest in his Divine Will, knowing by deep conviction and spiritual revelation, the wisdom of His great Plan and Purpose for the universe.

Thus did the *New Day* of October 2, 1965, announce an event for which followers could find explanation in their Father's own words. He had often warned that they may not always have a "God-in-a-body" with them, that he might test their faith, and that God is a spirit only temporarily resident in a body. Many perhaps did not hear or did not want to believe this. Mother reassured them that this act was Father's will and had a profound significance, when she announced immediately after his bodily death:

> I thank Father that each of you will move in Father's mind and spirit because I know everything is according as He Wills it . . . what Father did He did and is doing for the world. . . . As Father's spirit and body cannot be separated, we look for Him to arise, and let us watch in his mind and spirit; because nothing can harm Father. Father is all there is. Therefore He *has* the victory and *is* the victory, but we must be *with* Him if we are going to be with Him.

Mother recognized the difficulty many might have in parting with the visible symbol of their God. She went on to say:

> Now you must each hold to your own integrity, because it is understood that this will affect individuals according to their concept and consecration; but as Father has told us, keep your mind and your eyes on Him! Walk with your God. Know your God. There is nothing anyone can do to help another but live in Father's mind and spirit, because we have nothing to depend on and it is everything to depend on God's Holy Spirit. This is God's Day now! Man's day is out! We will shortly see how it is when His Spirit shakes the earth. He has given us all this year to prepare ourselves and we love Him for this peace that surpasses all understanding and nothing can disturb this knowledge that we are substantiated in.

Mother Divine referred to the fact that Father Divine had been under the care of a doctor and had been practically unable to appear in public for the last year. The followers had already come to accept the spiritual presence of Father without a physical presence, with the dwindling number of his appearances in public over the past few years. When he had appeared, it was either Mother who spoke for him, or a recording of one of his earlier messages. Followers were aware that they were to address Father through Mother, and the *New Day* had been reprinting messages delivered before 1960.

A rationale for Father's physical decline had been developing throughout these years of silence expressed in such statements as the one reprinted week after week in the *New Day*. It became the official explanation of Father's silence:

> In a recent communication in response to one exalting the beauty and life of His Words, Father Divine said,

> "You have often heard Me say, 'I need not say more'; and it is true. I have already spoken much more than fifty years in advance of our present civilization. Had I not done so humanity could not have been saved, for I have laid the cornerstone of a New Nation, not only conceived by God, but builded by Him. On the faith, on the hope, on the moral standards of virtue, honesty, competence and truth that I have exemplified, mankind is rebuilding the civilization that would have been lost as others have been."[1]

In May of 1960 the Philadelphia newspapers printed an account of Father Divine's illness in a suburban hospital. The official answer was a press release from "Father Divine's Office":

Woodmont, Friday, May 13, 1960 A.D.F.D.

In response to numerous phone calls and requests for information by the press concerning Father Divine, the following statement is released: Father Divine is alive, well, happy and carrying on His spiritual work. Father Divine is truly fulfilling the scripture:

"Fear not; I am the first and the last:
I am he that liveth and was (reported) dead; and behold I am alive forevermore, Amen; and I have the keys of h_____ and of death." (Revelation 1:17, 18)

Isaiah, the prophet spoke of this day:

"And he will destroy in this mountain the face of the covering cast over the people, and the veil that is spread over all nations.

"He will swallow up death in victory; and the Lord God will wipe away tears from off all faces; and the rebuke of his people shall he take away from all the earth; for the Lord hath spoken it.

"And it shall be said in that day, Lo, this is our God; we have waited for him, and he will save us: this is the Lord; we have waited for him, we will be glad and rejoice in his salvation." (Isaiah 25:7–9)

"He took upon Himself our infirmities and bore our sicknesses."

"The chastisement of our peace was upon him; and with his stripes we are healed." (Matt. 8:17 and Isa. 53:5)

Father has often said:

"It is not anything I do as a Person to reach any condition, but according to the faith of the individual matters are usually adjusted harmoniously and satisfactorily.

"With or without any body I am the same and I shall not cease My endeavors until I have it under My Personal jurisdiction and on My immediate staff, where all have the reality of life, of liberty and of happiness.

"The true followers all over the world of Father and Mother Divine are informed and in accord with whatsoever Father Divine's Spirit allows Him to do. We stand united in faith, in service, in consecration and devotion to Father and Mother Divine for we know he is God."

In this press release it was clear for the first time that someone other than Major J. Divine was speaking for Father Divine. Hitherto, in matters of faith, reporters had always been referred to Father himself or to his printed messages, and no questions had ever been answered except by quoting Father Divine's own words. Although the bulk of the statement was made up of quotations from the Bible or from Father Divine, his "office" had plainly made the selections and, in effect, was setting the standard that the true follower was to accept whatever happened to the body of Father Divine as having been willed by him as God. Mother Divine was to be accepted as deserving faith, service, consecration, and devotion.

It is at this point in the history of the Peace Mission Movement that schism and disintegration might have occurred. Some individuals may have lost their faith at this time, but many more seem to have reaffirmed theirs. Mother Divine was a strong leader in this process: She appeared at the daily Communion Service at Woodmont and, after the reading of one of Father's messages, added her testimony to that of various visitors from churches in the United States, Australia, Switzerland, and Panama.

On May 15, 1960, two days after the press release, Mother Divine spoke:

> Peace, Father Dear; Peace everyone. Father Dear, I rise to thank you for being just who you are, and I, at this time, especially want to thank you for your beautiful words of Spirit and Life that are so consoling, so strengthening, so uplifting, and they are that because they are truth! [So true, many listeners affirmed.] And I thank you for all of your true and faithful children throughout the world that love you more today than they have ever loved you. [Applause and cheers.] And I thank you, Father dear, for your long-suffering and patience that has established yourself in our hearts to reign in our hearts and minds. We have room for you! In the Sonship Degree there was no room in the Inn for the Christ Child. God, as He came in the Sonship Degree was a stranger to the earth plane; He was an alien; but I thank you, Father, for coming in the Father-ship Degree with the victory over every mind, over every negative condition in us and have prepared these bodies to receive you! And that is why today, the Mount of the House of the Lord stands as a beautiful material resting place for you, and I thank you from the very depths of my soul for this holy ground where your beautiful body now rests, right here in your home, that your love has prepared for you, and that we can come here and give you our hearts full of praise and adoration, and that you can personally hear it over the amplifying system. We are deeply grateful to you for this because we know that it is you who have done everything—that we are nothing; we can do nothing. But we thank you for the way you have unfolded yourself in us through your many sacrifices, and I know that is just what you are doing today—growing in us!

And I thank you that we love you tenderly, sweetly, and beyond measure as you are bringing to this world this brand new birth, and we are seeing not just the budding but the flowering of this new Heaven here on earth. I thank you, Father dear.[2]

This statement signified two essential processes in maintaining the faith and unity of Father Divine's followers. First was identification of his mission with a spiritual being rather than a bodily one, listening, though absent. Father Divine had always taught the importance of a spiritual presence, at the same time that he emphasized a practical God, interested in human beings' material needs.

The second process emphasized the symbol of God's material success. Woodmont was such a symbol. As Mother Divine said, "The Mount of the House of the Lord stands as a beautiful material resting place for you . . . this holy ground . . . your home . . . that we can come here and give you our hearts full of praise. . . ." It also symbolized the followers' love for Father Divine and his for them.

Father Divine had forged religious and cultural unity from the participation of many individuals in a common response to such symbols as were now being reinterpreted. The apparent break in continuity with the Father of the past was experienced as another transition rather than a break. Wherever Father Divine chose to take his body, his followers felt that there was a holy place; hence Woodmont, where he spent much of his time after 1953, became a symbol of his presence as it was of Mother's, who had been continuously at his side since 1946.

Her words, expressions of love for Father, and the biblical references, were typical of Father's own speech and of the emotional response it drew from his followers. Thus was a continuity maintained with the Father Divine of former years.

The highly ritualized style of everyday life continued, as well as symbols of word, place, and person. Followers continued to live in the same familiar surroundings, and with the same fellow followers. They participated in the same regular religious services several nights of the week and shared in the Communion table every day. Meanwhile their Father's words came to them on tape, in the *New Day*, and at the services several hours each day. The years from 1960 to 1965 must well have been a time of testing for those who could not accept a silent Father Divine, yet there was still a loyal following on the morning of September 10, 1965, when Mother announced, "This is God's day now."

Because followers are scattered about the world and the author had no way of observing them all, only those in the community centered around Philadelphia can be our measure of constancy. Among these, I am aware of no defections at the time of Mother Divine's succession. In any religious movement people do leave for one reason or another, and in the light of such a potentially disrupting event as the loss of the paramount leader, it seems logical that some dropout must have occurred.

But earlier writers' prophecies of suicides[3] and mass departures[4] were not fulfilled. The twenty-second Wedding Anniversary of Father and Mother Divine from April 27 to May 5, 1968, was celebrated by the same numerous followers seen there during several years of observation. Followers from New York, New Jersey, California, Australia, and Europe bused and flew in with about the same representation in numbers as they had ever since 1960. Allowing for the usual attrition in any group, familiar faces appear today (1978) as they did in 1968.

Although from this kind of research no definitive answer can be given to the question: "How is it that people keep their faith even in the light of apparent disconfirmation of a belief?" some discussion of it is appropriate and possible. Social psychologists Festinger, Riecken, and Schachter[5] have reported on their examination of the problem in connection with an American group that predicted the end of the world. They state their hypothesis:

> Suppose an individual believes something with his whole heart; suppose further that he has a commitment to this belief, that he has taken irrevocable actions because of it; finally, suppose that he is presented with evidence, unequivocal and undeniable evidence that his belief is wrong: what will happen? The individual will frequently emerge, not only unshaken, but even more convinced of the truth of his beliefs than ever before. Indeed he may even show a new fervor about convincing and converting other people to his view.

There are five conditions under which increased fervor might be expected:

1
A belief must be held with deep conviction and it must have some relevance to action, that is, to what the believer does or how he behaves.

2
The person holding the belief must have committed himself to it; that is for the sake of his belief, he must have taken some important action that is impossible to undo. In general, the more important such actions are, and the more difficult they are to undo, the greater is the individual's commitment to the belief.

3
The belief must be sufficiently specific and sufficiently concerned with the real world so that events may unequivocally refute the belief.

4
Such undeniable disconfirmatory evidence must occur and must be recognized by the individual holding the belief.

Deep conviction and commitment leading to important action (conditions 1 and 2) are certainly overwhelmingly present among Father Divine's followers and, according to Festinger, will make the belief resistant to change. It is open to question whether the belief in the persistence of Father Divine's body was really widely held. The alternative belief, that his nature was spiritual and as such was not dependent on his body, meets the specifications of condition 3, that the belief be sufficiently specific and sufficiently concerned with the real world that events may unequivocally refute the belief. In other words, did the followers believe specifically that their Father's *body* would never die or that his *spirit* would never die? And if so is there anything occurring in the real world which could unequivocally refute the belief? Did the stilling of Father Divine's body furnish "undeniable disconfirmatory evidence" and was it "recognized by the individual holding the belief" (condition 4)? According to Festinger, if conditions 3 and 4 are met, they

> would exert powerful pressure on a believer to discard his belief. It is of course possible that an individual, even though deeply convinced of a belief, may discard it in the face of unequivocal disconfirmation. We must, therefore, state a fifth condition specifying the circumstances under which the belief will be discarded and those under which it will be maintained with new fervor.

5
The individual believer must have social support. It is unlikely that one isolated believer could withstand the kind of disconfirming evidence we have specified. If, however, the believer is a member of a group of convinced persons who can support one another, we would expect the belief to be maintained and the believers to attempt to proselyte or to persuade nonmembers that the belief is correct.

This condition is certainly met by the followers' communal existence; any who might have felt their belief in the immortality of Father Divine's spirit shaken when his body was stilled, found social support for continued belief in his reiterated assurance that his spirit and mind would never leave them. A visit today with a group of the followers will verify that they are anxious to share their conviction that Father, in body and in spirit, is what they have always believed him to be: God, Father Divine. Any one of the almost nightly meetings of followers in Philadelphia or anywhere else in the world where they gather will yield testimonies such as Miss Priscilla Paul's, given in 1967, at a celebration of the twenty-first Wedding Anniversary:

"Peace FATHER, Peace MOTHER. Mr. and Mrs. Facenda" (a well-known Philadelphia television news reporter covering the meeting).

Angels of the Kingdom and Everyone: FATHER and MOTHER DIVINE, I am so proud to be here today and I am proud to see everyone else here as we are celebrating this wonderful occasion—the Marriage Anniversary of the BRIDE and the LAMB. It is truly Wonderful!

I thank FATHER and MOTHER to think about the first day that I saw FATHER DIVINE. I was brought to FATHER DIVINE—I had been discharged from Johns Hopkins Hospital a cripple. I had infantile paralysis and I was told that I would never walk again—but I can jump, hop, skip today! Wonderful! I thank YOU FATHER AND MOTHER DIVINE.

And I am proud to think of the different congregations that I have been in and heard them sing that my FATHER is rich in houses and lands, HE holdeth the wealth of the world in HIS hands; rubies, diamonds, silver and gold; HIS coffers are full, HE has riches untold. But I have thought that since I have known FATHER DIVINE and know what HE stands for and what HE does for people, what good would the riches—rubies, diamonds and gold—do for FATHER or me, either one, as long as HE was holding them? Now you can see HE's holding *us* and turning them a-loose. [Merriment and applause.] And I have also heard people sing, "Come over here where the Feast of the LORD is going on," and honestly, I was at a church one night and the people were so hungry they could hardly sing!—but today, look at the Feast of the LORD!—mental, spiritual, material—it is truly wonderful! And I thank FATHER DIVINE to know that HE is EVER PRESENT—that FATHER DIVINE hasn't gone any place. If HE had, all the blessings that are flowing would have terminated! ["So true," affirmed many in the audience.] But you can see that FATHER DIVINE is RIGHT HERE WITH US! FATHER has told us that with or without a body, it didn't make any difference with HIM, that HE was going to put this issue through, and you do see that's exactly what FATHER DIVINE is doing! It is so sweet and it is so beautiful! [Applause resounds.]

I recall we went down to register to get ready for voting in New York City and they didn't want to take our names because they didn't like the sound of them. [This was in the 1930s.] I went up to get FATHER to come down to the polls with me, and FATHER came down and HE told the man who was registering the people, "Now if you don't want MY Followers to vote they do not have to register nor vote, because I want you politicians to know that with or without the ballot, or the bullet, I'M going to put MY issue through!" [Thunderous applause and cheers resound in sanction of this.] And we are not using the ballot, not the kind that people usually use, and we are not using the bullet, but FATHER DIVINE. We know, we realize this—it is in our hearts and minds, we are not just talking—that the government is really upon FATHER DIVINE'S Shoulders, and FATHER Said years ago, when many of you had not even heard of FATHER DIVINE, "As it is here on MY immediate Staff," which was integrated, "I AM going to have it like this all over the world!" And HE said, "Way down in Texas, in the furthest parts of the south"—and that's where FATHER got Mr. Lyndon Baines Johnson from—way down in Texas!—and FATHER said, "You are going to attend the same schools, you are going to worship in the same pews, you are going to ride on the same cars, buses and planes." And we are doing that today! [Thunderous applause.]

Now I'm not going to take up a lot of time but just think about, when I was brought to FATHER DIVINE I had absolutely nothing, and from rags to riches, in the Name of GOD FATHER DIVINE I stand today! I thank YOU FATHER and MOTHER.[6]

These convictions of Father Divine's continued activity, "with or without a body," stressed the same areas of emotional and physical needs which had confirmed his charisma in earlier years. Recovery from infantile paralysis and the speaker's present vigor were attributed to Father Divine—He who had fed the multitudes, who had instituted integration in his own staff, and predicted that it would occur even in the South, placing a Southerner in the White House to carry out that prediction. He had taken his followers from "rags to riches."

It seems accurate to say that as of May 1968, Father Divine's charisma for thousands of followers had not died. They sang, reinforcing their conviction:

FATHER is still in the driver's seat,
HE is holding the reins,
HE is steering the wheel,
And all HIS Words are being fulfilled,
HE has declared long years ago
"With or without MY Bodily Form
I shall Rule and Reign forever
And I'll never leave you alone!"

In this period of transition from an embodied God to an ethereal one, Mother Divine's role as the person who had been closest to Father Divine, was primarily of reassurance for the future. Nothing could harm Father, "he will arise" and "his Spirit will shake the world." In her words and actions she exemplified unshaken faith in the continued mind, spirit, principles, and leadership of Father Divine.

By marriage designated as the supreme symbol of the virtues which Father Divine preached to the followers, she constantly represented the significance of that marriage.

Kitty Blue, a columnist for the *New Day,* wrote in the May 4, 1968, issue of the joys of spring and the Wedding Anniversary, which was then being celebrated in all the churches:

> If joy has come to the world, a supernal fountain of happiness has come to the followers of the Lamb and His dear Bride.
>
> This, for us also, is the season of resurrection and revitalization. We realize that Christ is being resurrected within us daily. Is not this the reason He came? It is also the season of revitalization because we reflect more markedly on virtue, the most potent attribute of God. Is not this the reason for the Marriage of FATHER and MOTHER DIVINE?
>
> This is life and if we see with the eyes of the spirit, we might reflect; the dawn of the millennium is here! The long hard struggle under the curse of disobedience imposed in the Garden of Eden has passed and the warmth of the sun of God's Bodily Presence and the renewing of the soft rains of sacrifice that wash our souls and make us grow, tells us that it is Spring. GOD has come and wed His creation. . . . Christ rises resurrected within man and he becomes once more, the son of GOD, not in one body called Jesus alone, but in every one who nurtures the conviction that FATHER DIVINE is GOD and that MOTHER DIVINE is the model of the perfect life.
>
> FATHER DIVINE GOD ALMIGHTY. I know I speak for every one of your loved ones when I say I thank You for the honor and privilege of knowing You are GOD, of seeing You face to face, of coming before You to be purged of all sin and going forward with a free heart and a clean body and of giving You thenceforth all my love. Give me the courage and strength and grace to bear Your Great Name in humility and to sacrifice my life and my all to the Cause of the establishment of heaven on earth.
>
> MOTHER DIVINE, Exemplar of this noble Church without spot or wrinkle, I pledge to YOU and to FATHER every capability that I possess because YOU stand undaunted in His Will and because YOU Both love us so.
>
> Happy Anniversary in and to this dawn of a new day, a new Spring and a new world of utopia which we now possess and which is for all the world in time to come!

Mother is looked to now (1978) as the physical embodiment of leadership of the Movement, though followers still stress that Father is always present and she invariably prefaces her remarks to the followers with a greeting to Father. In a *New Day* report of a visit by a group of students and faculty from a Bible Institute, dated April 17, 1968, the editor says: FATHER and MOTHER DIVINE Personally served them, and at this time MOTHER arose to explain the Service, speaking as follows: 'Peace FATHER, Peace Everyone.'"

In the process of welcoming the guests and explaining the Communion and devotional service about to begin, Mother Divine emphasized Father Divine's significance and what he preached and practiced:

> We thank YOU, FATHER, for all that YOU have done to make religion practical—to tangibilate and materialize spiritual things and spiritualize material things, that our whole life could be that which is of GOD. We shouldn't just worship GOD on Sunday and on the other days do what we want to do, but like in the Peace Mission, we live in our Churches. Our activities are all within the Churches or based on what we would consider would be Evangelical, and our whole concept of thinking is based on the REALITY of GOD with us. GOD is our FATHER and we are HIS Children! We thank YOU, FATHER, for this Family that is not confined to the Peace Mission Movement, to those who call themselves Followers of YOURS, but includes all those that are patterning their lives after that of the Holiness of JESUS and the Virginity of MARY—all who are pursuing RIGHTEOUSNESS, JUSTICE and TRUTH.[7]

In June of 1977 at their annual business meetings various churches in the Movement voted to change their By-Laws to include the charismatic status of Mother Divine with a statement about church leadership.[8] The original By-Law, "The Pastor, REVEREND M. J. DIVINE, better known as FATHER DIVINE, as Author and Finisher of our Faith, Whose Name shall be called Wonderful, Counsellor, Mighty GOD, Everlasting FATHER and King of Peace, according to the Scripture, shall be the Supreme Spiritual Authority in all things," was changed to read:

> The Pastor, REVEREND M. J. DIVINE, Ms.D., D.D., better known as FATHER DIVINE, as Author and Finisher of our Faith, Whose Name shall be called Wonderful, Counsellor, Mighty GOD, Everlasting FATHER and King of Peace, according to the Scripture; and HIS SPOTLESS VIRGIN BRIDE, MRS. M. J. DIVINE, better known as MOTHER DIVINE, Symbolizing the Universal Church without Spot and without Blemish, shall be the Supreme Spiritual Authority in all things.

In presenting this motion for the change in the By-Laws many statements of
Father Divine's were invoked referring to Mother Divine's charismatic nature.
Some cited at this meeting were:

> MY BRIDE has so absorbed MY Life, MY Nature and My Characteristics
> in Her Consciousness and in Her Life that She has become ONE with ME. I
> say of Her in this FATHERHOOD Dispensation as I said of JESUS in the
> SONSHIP, "This is MY beloved SON in Whom I AM well pleased" (*New
> Day*, 5/10/53, p. 34).

> For this cause as I was saying this afternoon, you say I AM the HEAD of
> the Church, but we are happy to say, as a Spiritual HEAD, "She stands with
> ME!" (*New Day*, 3/1/52, p. 14).

> GOD is Ever Present with you. When I AM Personally absent, you know as
> those in Australia, in Switzerland, in New Zealand and in all parts of the
> world—they know I AM there and they recognize the Presence of MOTHER
> DIVINE and MYSELF COMBINED as the HEAD of the Church in all
> parts of the world. Aren't you glad! (*New Day*, 9/23/50, p. 16).

> MY BRIDE is not a woman after the manner of women, but She is an AN-
> GEL, a Chosen ANGEL to be MY BRIDE, and Her Life of Virginity is held
> sacred by all who have the Spirit of CHRIST in their hearts.... So then, one
> who speaks against MY SPOTLESS VIRGIN BRIDE speaks against the
> HOLY GHOST, for the HOLY GHOST which is the Spirit of Truth, is
> within Her (*New Day*, 8/26/50, p. 29).

> Since I have made MY SPOTLESS ANGEL, MY SPOTLESS VIRGIN
> BRIDE—by this Mental and Spiritual Connection, thinking harmoniously
> together, I carry MOTHER with ME wheresoever We go, and I bless the
> people through MOTHER even as I did through JESUS—FOR THAT IS
> THE MYSTERY (*New Day*, 5/10/52, p. 4).

Again FATHER says of Mother Divine:

> BEHOLD THE VIRTUE! I say, BEHOLD THE VIRTUE! behold the
> virginity! behold the unity! behold the tranquility! BEHOLD THE GODLI-
> NESS AND BEHOLD MY DEITY! Aren't you glad!

> VISION THE VIRTUE AND THE HOLINESS AND THE HONESTY.
> VISION THE DECENCY AND COMPETENCE AND TRUTH! VISION
> THE HOLINESS OF MARY AND THE HOLINESS OF JESUS. VISION
> THE VIRGINITY OF MARY AND THE HOLINESS OF JESUS UNITED!

By this, we shall have a Righteous Government, for this is MY RIGH-
TEOUS CHURCH, a CHURCH Depicted in ONE! As I declared, A GLO-
RIOUS CHURCH WITHOUT SPOT AND WITHOUT BLEMISH!
(*New Day,* 5/1/48).

At this meeting Mother Divine expressed her conviction about her responsibility
to Father Divine and to the followers:

Peace, FATHER, Peace, Everyone! I just wanted to make a statement in
answer to what—[one person] said to the effect that I would be, well, Supreme Authority, and would be telling everybody else what to do and also
that the ones who have specific duties and offices, wouldn't be functioning
in their same capacity. I don't think anyone but FATHER has stressed so
much about everyone being governed by their own highest intuition as I
have. I feel in fulfilling the MOTHERSHIP Degree that FATHER has endowed Me with, I can perceive the CHRIST coming to fruition in the different individuals and I can protect them and guide them in the direction
that they should go in order to bring it to fruition. [Loud applause resounds.]
And that's one reason why I think FATHER married Me so that the CHRIST
could be protected that IT might come to fruition in many bodies, because if
I AM not in this position or Am not recognized, either the self in you is
going to be recognized or some other personality who is not gifted or given
the blessing of that ability that FATHER gave Me, and I AM CLAIMING
IT! [Thunderous and dynamic applause resounds.] Thank YOU, FATHER
Dear.

Mother spoke at some length about the spiritual progress of the followers and
concluded:

Many of us think that we are Followers of FATHER DIVINE and representing Him, when we are far from it! And not a one can point their finger
at another one! Then if we all know it, then we should all get ourselves out
of the way and give FATHER THE RIGHT OF WAY and give FATHER
the HONOR; and FATHER says you should be willing to see CHRIST in
somebody else more than yourself! And I'm sure if FATHER saw it in Me,
I think some of you ought to be able to see it to help Me to be it. [Thunder-
ous and dynamic applause sanctions this remark.]

I sure want to help each one of you to be what you should be. I want to honor
the Calling that FATHER has given to each one of you. I can't fill everybody's duty and everybody's office! I don't want to. I have my Office just like
FATHER said HE had HIS Office! And I'm not trying to fill FATHER
DIVINE'S Office, but FATHER has to use bodies and I enjoy seeing dif-

ferent ones come into their real Calling, to the place that GOD has called them to.

And we had much experience in the different ones coming to be co-workers. You may want someone to fill a certain position, you may feel that they are qualified, but unless it's the Will of the Spirit and their Calling, it just does not work out! And what is coming into reality now, I mean REALITY, is the UNIFIED BODY OF CHRIST of many Members, each according to his particular calling, the hand, the feet, the head, everything is coming together and we all are—we all have our particular calling and it's all essential. Each one is necessary and I want to be able to see it in each one and respect it in each one. And as we are going to be this Unified Body of CHRIST where we can be really ONE MAN AT JERUSALEM, where we can pluck one string and the whole Heaven can ring! And in this Unified Body of CHRIST, FATHER and I happen to be the HEAD! [Dynamic applause resounds.]

I do thank YOU, FATHER Dear, for being GOD and for YOUR great PLAN and your great PURPOSE. And I know that this is no one day's journey. We have been coming with FATHER since before time began. We have sung and we realize we were with FATHER when HE moved out upon the face of the deep and brought everything into expression. So we have nothing to think about but to just go on with FATHER. To really know GOD for ourselves as I told every one of you when FATHER laid HIS BODY down, that you all had to know GOD for yourself. And I say the same thing today.

I Am not wanting to have the responsibility of telling you this and telling you that, but I Am interested in you moving in the right direction and seeing that you are learning to listen to the Spirit and to abide in the MIND of FATHER DIVINE. And I feel that now we are going to demand it more of ourselves as individuals, and in doing so, we will automatically represent it more as a group or as a Church, and it's only as we can produce this CHRIST that we are to be the LIGHT that FATHER IS. FATHER is the LIGHT of the WORLD, but the world sees FATHER through us. We want FATHER to be HIM in REALITY, so that the MAGNETISM that FATHER IS can draw HIS Own unto HIM, that the earth might be blessed by HIS PRESENCE and the Kingdom of GOD might be a UNIVERSAL REALITY ON EARTH. Thank YOU FATHER Dear.

This is an appropriate point at which to return to the theory of charismatic leadership, especially as it is reflected in Mother Divine's role in the Movement.

In Weber's theory of charisma a key indicator was that a small group of followers formed around the leader "based on an emotional form of communal leadership." Such were Father Divine's Secretaries and the Rosebuds, among whom Mother Divine was paramount.

In economic relationships, the Divine community had already developed enough of a status and role structure to maintain its growth and survival. Despite its role and status, which made the Movement economically compatible with the laws, values, and mores of the larger society, Father Divine's Heaven on Earth and Holy Family might never have come about if he had not given it leadership and social organization. This happened as one stage in a process which Weber calls the "routinization of charisma." Without the charisma of Father Divine such a group of individuals would never have interacted; their association with the "body" of their God formed the organization called the Peace Mission Movement.

With a secure and ongoing way of life routinized through Father Divine's appointment of Secretaries, Rosebuds, Lily-Buds, and Crusaders—who therefore shared in his charisma, with provision made for election of officers for formally organized church groups, the community could continue indefinitely.

Certain followers' financial status today is completely dependent upon the organization. They work in the physical maintenance of the buildings, are co-owners of businesses under the Peace Mission label—including the hotels, churches, missions, and apartments owned by those who live in them—or the older people who no longer work but have invested their money in these same properties. These will continue to be the core of followers whose ideal and material interests keep them actively concerned with maintaining the community. Without this mundane involvement some followers might attach their spiritual anchor to a new charismatic figure or, finding material security in the larger society, abandon the attempt to maintain a charismatic community. Those with financial involvement may either continue to "spiritualize" their material investments, as the Shakers have, they may incorporate as a business as the Oneida Community of Perfectionists did,[9] or take some other course.

In other groups under charismatic leadership those most interested in continuing the community organization with its status relationships become conspicuous when the leader has disappeared and the problem of succession is unresolved. The survival of the charismatic group and the character of future social relationships depend on how well these uncertainties are settled.

Weber suggests five principal types of solution to the problem of the succession of leadership.[10] Mother Divine would appear to have assumed leadership by two of these means. Through her marriage to Father Divine she was set apart and

accepted as a symbol of all that he preached. One of Weber's five means is se-
lection of the new leader by the original charismatic leader. The second means is
by heredity, or through the passage of charisma to a close relative; this, like the
first, would apply in the case of Mother Divine, his wife. Father and Mother
Divine's charisma was shared by several Secretaries who were always accorded a
position of "closeness" to Father and Mother Divine, both physically by always
accompanying them and occupying the closest seats at Communions, and socio-
logically by the responsibilities they carried for the conduct of the communal life
and the religious services.

For the foreseeable future neither Father Divine's charisma nor the charismatic
group which formed around him is likely to fade out. A viable form of social organization is there, with a dedicated, experienced staff of followers. The problem
of succession has been met: with his body and spirit still available to the true believer, a charismatic Mother Divine, and certain Secretaries function at the center
of an efficient church organization capable of handling problems of everyday
social life.

We cannot completely answer the question with which we started the quest:
"What are the social conditions under which charismatic leadership emerges and
flowers and dies?" In this instance charismatic leadership has not died for some
thousands of believers spread around the globe.

In the concluding chapter we shall discuss the social conditions in which, in this
instance at least, charismatic leadership emerged and flourished.

X

Conclusion

The author accepts the premise that a religious leader cannot be explained apart from his cultural and social setting or without some understanding of the culture base on which his appeal rests. As Hoult says, such a person is part of a "certain concatenation of cultural forces and historical circumstances without which . . . [he] might live and die unnoticed."[1] "He is part of a complicated causal nexus," according to Yinger.[2] His complex influence is intertwined with the interests, needs, and tendencies of those with whom he interacts. Some will reject him and others will respond positively in different ways.

Weber holds that charismatic leaders appear in times of distress—psychic, physical, economic, ethical, religious, or political distress. They have been neither officeholders nor incumbents of an "occupation" in the sense that they have expert knowledge and work for remuneration. Often the charismatic leader addresses himself to a group of persons whose existence is delimited either locally, socially, politically, or occupationally, or in some other way.

> Charisma knows only inner determination and inner restraint. The holder of charisma seizes the task that is adequate to him and demands obedience and a following by virtue of his mission. His success depends on whether he finds them. If they recognize him, he is their master—so long as he knows how to maintain recognition through "proving" himself . . . those who faithfully surrender to him must fare well.[3]

Father Divine's initial impact on large numbers of people came during the depression in the midst of economic and political distress. Without claiming any professional training in job placement, medicine, psychotherapy, or theology he promised by supernatural means to cure distress in all of these areas. He promised to minister to anyone, but especially to those who came from a minority in our society. And he "proved" himself to those who were satisfied that through him they had found an answer to their distress.

Sociologists have held that the condition of the larger society around them is a factor in individuals' personal distress, and that social and psychological conditions favor the development of charismatic movements.

Parsons holds that "any situation where an established institutional order has to a considerable extent become disorganized, where established routines, expectations, and symbols are broken up or under attack is a favorable situation for such a movement."[4] Such a situation produces widespread psychological insecurity, which may be resolved by participation in a charismatic movement.

Wallis, who investigated forty-nine Jewish, forty-nine Muslim, and forty-six Christian "messiahs" appearing over the last twenty centuries, comes to the conclusion that:

> The messiah imparts faith and courage to a wavering people, and bolsters a culture which seems to be tottering to a fall. Generally he calls upon his people to do something about their troubles, and their circumstances. If he can galvanize them into action, he can make them shake off their lethargy and live more zealously, or at least preface failure with purpose. Action is a solvent of despair."[5]

Both Parsons and Wallis indicate that a charismatic leader and movement appear at a time of breakdown in the cultural structure. Elaborating on Durkheim, Merton has called this breakdown in the cultural structure *anomie.*

Merton holds that human environment involves the cultural structure on the one hand and the social structure on the other, and that no matter how closely connected these are, for purposes of analysis they must be kept separate.

> Cultural structure may be defined as that organized set of normative values governing behavior which is common to a designated society or group [and] social structure is . . . that organized set of social relationships in which members of the society or groups are variously implicated.

> Anomie is then conceived as a breakdown in the cultural structure, occurring particularly when there is an acute disjunction between the cultural norms and goals and the socially structured capacities of members of the group to act in accord with them.[6]

The cultural structure of the United States contains the widely voiced norms of equal treatment for all persons, but social relationships are actually based on discrimination by race, and sometimes religion and sex. Certainly many Americans of darker complexions or minority religions or females or of low income have been caught up in a condition of anomie, as defined by Merton. The capacity to compete for education, jobs, and self-respect is limited by the fact that discrimination has made it impossible to achieve the cultural norms of self-support and equal treatment. It was to this group that Father Divine made his initial appeal.

A number of adaptive reactions to anomie, as described by Merton, are: delinquency, crime, suicide, innovation, retreatism, and rebellion.

For some people caught in an anomic situation, Father Divine provided an opportunity for rebellion and the adoption of new norms. "When rebellion is confined to relatively small groups and relatively powerless elements in a community, it provides a potential for the formation of subgroups, alienated from the rest of the community but unified within themselves."[7]

Thus "the kingdom of Father Divine" may be described as a subgroup, with its own culture—perhaps one that is peculiarly American—and also as an example of rebellion against anomie, against a disorganized culture and society.

Indeed, Parsons notes that our society is particularly susceptible to charismatic movements. He cites Christian Science, Buchmanism, and the Peace Mission as examples of such movements.

Certainly, minority group members are subject to anomie, distress, frustration, and strain if they take the "American Creed" literally for, as Ralph Bunche observes:

> Every man in the street, white, black, red or yellow, knows that this is the "land of the free," the "land of opportunity," the "cradle of liberty," the "home of democracy," that the American flag symbolizes the "equality of all men" and guarantees to us all "the protection of life, liberty and property," freedom of speech, freedom of religion and racial tolerance.[9]

Yet, as Myrdal puts it,

> The influences from the American Creed have a double direction. On the one hand the Creed operates directly to make people's thoughts more and more "independent of race, creed or color," as the American slogan runs. On the other hand, it indirectly calls forth the same dogma of inferiority to justify the exception of the Negro to the Creed. The need for race prejudice is, from this point of view, a need for defense on the part of Americans against their own national creed. . . . There is a great struggle in white people's minds—the struggle between the democratic ideals of equality in the American Creed and the obvious lack of equality in the treatment of the American Negro. This struggle we have called "an American dilemma."[10]

The "structured source" of strain and frustration for many if not all dark-skinned persons and for some if not many light-skinned persons, is the segregated social system in which they have lived. Neither "race" could really interact as status equals either in the North or the South; yet the widely held values of the American Creed hold up equality as an ideal. Exponents of religion (although perhaps in a minority) have referred to the Fatherhood of God and the brotherhood of man as an interracial or nonracial family; yet Loescher could report in 1948 that the Christian church was the most highly segregated institution in the United States.[11]

One miracle or "supernatural act" which contributed to Father Divine's charisma was his achievement of complete equality in his "holy family." His followers today believe that they long have practiced what they sing:

> The Kingdom it has come, and the will is being done;
> All men have been brought together and unified in one.
> No more separation, for God Himself has come and He is
>   reigning now.
>
> No races, creeds or colors shall be known here in this land;
> We shall be united in just one big band!
> God Himself is ruling, for the time is out for man
> Since God is ruling now.

A segregated social system has meant "unequal access" to economic benefits, yet the value system of the larger society teaches all Americans to expect to work for a living and that success in work may be a proof of religious attainment, perhaps salvation.[12] Many Americans believe from experience that their skin color determines whether they are to be the last hired and the first fired, regardless of the quality of their work. Another of Father Divine's miracles was his affirmation of the religious virtue of consistent hard work, and his seeming ability to put all of his followers to work. The discussion of "overcoming the depression" describes the methods used to accomplish this end.

Interracial marriage has been severely frowned on in American society; a mythology of unbridled sexuality which has grown up around the minority race has been used to justify and reinforce separation of the races. Frazier explains the disorganization of lower-class Afro-American family life as the result "of the impact of social and economic forces on the simple family organization which evolved in the rural South." Among these social forces are urbanization and mass migration to the segregated sections of northern cities.[13]

Father Divine's followers created a "holy family" which denies participation in overt sexuality and creates a "substitute family" based on the strictest of moral codes. Persons of all shades of complexion worship, work, eat, and live together, demonstrating that racial propinquity need not mean sexual aggression. And, most miraculous of all, Father Divine married "his spotless virgin bride" and continually reminded the world that she remained a virgin.

Father Divine was aware of the difficulties many Americans were experiencing in family life. His cure was a drastic one: do not get married or, if married, return to the state of mind and practice where all men are brothers and all women sisters, and all are the spiritual children of Father Divine. His cure for sexual promiscuity was to remove temptation by limiting social contact between the sexes and to practice complete celibacy.

He taught that many should not be allowed to propagate because of their "inhuman animalistic characteristics" and their poverty. "It would be a law that they would not and should not be allowed to propagate, so long as they are unclean and live in lacks, and wants and limitations, to bring into the world children to increase crime, immodesty, immorality, and everything else that is against the advancement of moral betterment."[14]

Further than this, ". . . it is foolish for any person who is underprivileged to continue to increase and multiply, to bring misery, disappointment and failure into the world and cause such as being termed your own flesh and blood to suffer the brutality of barbarism and the mistreatment by the overprivileged and oppressors of the people."[15]

He pictured abstention from propagation as a kind of strike against mistreatment of the poor and of minorities by the "overprivileged" and the "barbarians":[16]

> When the country itself—I mean the United States of America—will give everyone his equal rights and guarantee them individually, severally and collectively according to the Constitution and every person social equality from every angle expressible—then and only then will I release my claim on the hearts and minds and the bodies of the children of men! Then and only then will I allow propagation to start in its effects again, when every man shall have his equal rights in this country, when he will no longer be underprivileged and non-privileged.[17]

He stated that "sex has more force over the human life than anything else, with the exception of God,"[18] but without having experienced "a new birth of freedom under God," propagation will produce only "all sorts of inferiority, ailments and complaints" among the children. Ninety-nine and ninety-nine-hundredths percent of people are not fit to be parents. "There are too many wicked people increasing and multiplying and continuing to overpopulate . . . the earth with more wickedness, with more graft and with more greed and with more vice and with more crime of every kind."[19]

A final argument against marriage and reproduction was that "the poor class are the ones of every nation that are fooled by the war lords and others, to teach them how to propagate for the purpose of leading them into slaughter."[20]

Father assured his followers that by living in celibacy they would help to "propagate" the solution to the problems of immorality and insecurity in the world. They were convinced that the charges of sexual immorality and irresponsible parenthood could never be leveled at them, that this would contribute to the society Father envisaged, since they were "exemplars" of this perfect Christian democracy. Thus did some escape from the anomic and disorganized family life which is a part of the American scene, not only among the poor and the minority groups, but among other classes as well. They were convinced by Father Divine that their sacrifices would be rewarded by personal salvation, happiness, and perhaps even eternal life on this earth.

This, then, was the social and cultural setting in which Father Divine found his followers: the major institutions were disorganized in that government was not assuring equal treatment to all despite the ideal culture traits embodied in the Bill of Rights and the Constitution; the economic system was not providing enough employment for all, and this lack fell particularly on minority group members and the previously underprivileged; the family was a difficult unit to maintain because of disorganization in both economic and governmental institutions, as well as the problems attendant on migration to the city; and religious institutions did not meet the needs of people caught in this anomic situation.

At this point in the analysis it is useful to introduce the concept of "the definition of the situation." W. I. Thomas observed that:

> preliminary to any self-determined act of behavior there is always a stage of examination and deliberation which we may call "the definition of the situation." And actually not only concrete acts are dependent on the definition of the situation, but gradually a whole life-policy and the personality of the individual himself follow from a series of such definitions. But the child is always born into a group of people among whom all the general types of situation which may arise have already been defined and corresponding rules of conduct developed, and where he has not the slightest chance of making his definitions and following his wishes without interference.[21]

> The definition of the situation, is begun by the parents, . . . is continued by the community . . . and is formally represented by the school, the law, the church.[22]

Human behavior can be understood only when it is placed in its whole context, which in any situation includes both the objective verifiable "facts" as described by an uninvolved observer, and also the *meaning,* or how the situation *seems* to exist to the person experiencing the situation. The subjective meaning to the actor, his personal "definition of the situation," cannot be overlooked in interpreting human behavior since, as W. I. Thomas codified a theorem long held by serious thinkers, "If men define situations as real, they are real in their consequences."[23]

Early in his career Father Divine discovered that some people defined his participation in their lives as a supernatural event. Inherent in the culture to which Americans have all been exposed, and which has defined the situation in religious terms, is the admonition, perhaps not always accepted, that God intervenes in human affairs. And for Christians, God had already appeared in the body of Jesus and, for some, millenarianism or *chiliasm* holds that Christ in person will return to earth to reign for a thousand years. The *Parousia* or second coming of Christ is foretold in the Book of Revelations; belief in it has waxed and waned in Western culture ever since the first century A.D.[24] Various sects of the Middle Ages expected the Parousia, and the Reformation Anabaptists welcomed Christ's return. Mystics and Quietists in France and the Fifth Monarchy men in England gambled their lives on the appearance of Christ as a person. Later Sweden contributed the faith of Emmanuel Swedenborg, which, after his death, found expression in the Church of the New Jerusalem in England, the United States, and other countries. In the early nineteenth century the Rev. Edward Irving left the Presbyterians to found the Catholic Apostolic Church, which still waits fervently for the Second Advent. It may be surprising to some to recall that Sir Isaac Newton was a millenarian, as was Charles Wesley, one of the founders of Methodism. William Miller in the United States noted from the Book of Daniel that Christ would set up an earthly kingdom in 1843 or 1844.[25] Seventh Day Adventist churches, with over a half-million members all over the world, grew out of his conviction and still wait for the second coming.[26] Millenarianism, the second coming of God on earth, is far from lost in the definition of the situation held by many Christians throughout the world and in the United States.

Father Divine is sometimes designated as the Messiah, as well as the second coming of Christ and the Father of Christ. In its Christian version Messianism accepted Christ as the Messiah, whereas among historic Jews it was the belief that at God's discretion a personal Messiah, descended from King David, would free the Jews from foreign rule and restore an ideal kingdom in Palestine with Jerusalem as its capital. Throughout the centuries Jews have appeared who believed that they were the Messiah. Wallis listed forty-nine of them.[27] They include Bar-Cocheba who led a revolt against Rome in A.D. 135, David Alroy in the twelfth century, David Reubeni in the sixteenth, and Sabbatai Zevi who proclaimed himself the Messiah in Smyrna in 1665. Although Reform Jews have little interest in the Messiah, the concept is still a part of the culture, the definition of the situation of many Orthodox Jews. Some of the Jews in Father's following conceive of him as the Messiah; hence the slogan, in part, "Americanism, Democracy, Christianity, and Judaism are Synonymous." Father Divine identified individual freedom to support one's self and to worship as one wishes with the terms "Americanism and Democracy" and insisted that he (or his spirit) will ultimately bring freedom and equality in every land, just as the Messiah was to free the Jews.

Given the culture base of Americans and Europeans and those influenced by them throughout the world, it is possible to see that in religious terms the definition of the situation concerning the place of God in the universe contains the possibility that God might choose to appear through a son as he once did in Jesus, in a Messiah (who is still expected by some Jews and has arrived for others), or even in any body he chooses. Father Divine built on this prior "definition of the situation." "If God has appeared in a body before why shouldn't he do it again?" he asked. He also utilized W. I. Thomas's theorem that "if men define situations as real, they are real in their consequences." He expressed this in many different phrases. In fact, Father Divine became the principal definer of the situation, working with the culture traits already present in the childhood and religious training of his listeners. Who has not heard that God is always with you, that God has always existed, that there are mysteries which only God can explain? Even if these ideas are not entirely believed, everyone has heard them, and some may try to define a situation of discomfort or confusion in terms of them.

Father Divine's message of July 30, 1936, illustrates such a definition of the situation. As with many of his messages it starts with rhythm and Father Divine sings the introduction:

> Oh rise in the Light of the Words I have said,
> Rise and walk in the Light of My Word,
> Rise and shine, rise and shine.

> This is the way, it is the Truth and the Light,
> I have come to lead you right:
> I'll lead you by day, and I'll teach you by night,
> Keep on walking in the Light of MY Love.

> Rise and shine, rise and shine, for thy Light has come,
> Rise and shine, rise and shine,
> Keep on walking in the Light of MY Love.

> You have heard what the Spirit said,
> Rise and shine, rise and shine,
> It is another mystery I Am going to reveal,
> Keep on walking in the Light of MY Love!

> Rise and shine, etc.

GOD is your FATHER, there is no other one,
Rise and shine, etc.
Keep on walking in the Light of MY Word!

You should never doubt a Word I say,
Rise and shine, etc.

This was a message from the heart of one;
You have heard it, and now you sing;
Another new mystery I Am going to explain,
Keep on walking in the Light of MY Word!

Rise and shine, etc.

Lo, I have been with you all along the way,
I came to teach you by night and day,
I came to show you the Holy way,
Keep on walking in the Light of MY Word!

Father spoke as follows:

Peace Everyone! Again I sit and again I stand, again I speak and again I sing.
MY Voice will be heard among all mankind through compositions, through
songs, through praises, through poems, and especially through rhythm,
whensoever speaking is heard.

The coming generation (if there be any) they will think and they will believe and they will understand, as to say, "they will see," such as others firstly
have not seen. . . . Before your conversion you could not see what you are
now observing, the things I have revealed to you. . . . Then I say,

"Rise and shine, rise and shine.
You should never doubt a Word I say,
Rise and shine, rise and shine,
And keep on walking in the Light of MY Word."

MY Words are filled with the Spirit of GOD'S Magneticness, they will attract you and will draw you nearer and nearer together. They will light up
your understanding. . . . They will attract your attention and draw your
minds . . . in this direction, for they are so far reaching they are convincing
to the most skeptic. The most skeptic person you ever saw or heard, to them
MY Words will be made plain, for they are understandable.[28]

Father Divine explained that hitherto the final interpreter of the meaning of life had not come. He will "take away the sins and the confusion of the world" and interpret "things that had been bewildering you and wool-gathering you without an interpretation." "For," he said:

> your Interpreter had not yet come until I came to you, things were not plain until I came! But the assertion, yea the statement is fulfilled this day in your hearing; "God is His Own interpreter, and He will make it plain."

> I am showing you the way to go Home! . . . Humanity and humanity's descendants have been drunk for five thousand, nine hundred and forty-two long years, since they were driven from the Presence of God in Adam in the Garden of Eden! [Here Father Divine is referring to Bishop Ussher's chronology which holds that the creation of the world took place in 4004 B.C.] I am showing them the way to go home! [The Book of Revelations] declared things that we are now fulfilling. How glorious it is to observe the mystery and to be in this Age and at this Time when God among you, through His Condescension, is with you as the Fulfiller . . . of the Scripture.[29]

Appendix A

Summary of the Peace Mission Movement Tenets

as published in the *New Day*, March 8, 1967

Politically

1

We are Americans. We believe in the Declaration of Independence and the Constitution, with its Bill of Rights and Amendments.

2

We are interracial, interdenominational, nonsectarian and nonpartisan. WE believe that every man has the inalienable right to vote and worship according to the dictates of his own conscience.

3

We live Father Divine's International Modest Code:
No smoking. No drinking. No obscenity. No vulgarity. No profanity. No undue mixing of the sexes. No receiving of gifts, presents, tips, or bribes.
We believe this code is fundamental to achieving national and world unity.

4

We believe that all men and nations should be independent. They should pay all just debts and return all stolen goods or the equivalent. This includes:
a
Restitution by individual nations for all territories taken by force.
b
Restitution by all individuals of mobs for all damage, injury or looting by the mob.

Socially

1

We are all equal to and independent of each other in the sight of God.

2

We believe that all men are entitled to not only equal treatment but the same inalienable rights to Life, Liberty and the Reality of Happiness.

3

We believe that self-control is birth control.

4

We believe that nothing good will be restrained from man to do when all live together in the Unity of the Spirit, of Mind, of Aim and of Purpose.

5

We believe that all men, who are worthy to live, shall live well, with the abundance of every comfort and convenience that modern society can produce.

6

We believe that every man has the responsibility to protect his fellowmen from being denied any right or freedom guaranteed by the Constitution.

7

We believe that all members of a mob, which commits murder should receive the full penalty of the law for first-degree murder. Also that the county wherein the crime is committed should pay not less than $10,000 to the deceased.

Educationally

1

We believe in the Public School System.

2

We believe that the doors of all educational institutions should be open and free for universal education with the same rights for all to higher education and professional training, according to ability.

3

We believe that English is the Universal Language and should be compulsory in the educational institutions of all nations.

4

We believe that a man is a man and not a so-called race, color or creed.

a

Therefore we have deleted from all books in the Peace Mission Free Schools and recommend abolishing in all educational institutions every qualifying adjective that tends to low-rate or produce inequality between men and men. We do not use expressions such as N-people, C-people, or W-people.

Economically

1

We live cooperatively. We individually cooperate to purchase, own and manage all our possessions in the best interest of humanity generally. Those who maintain these cooperative properties work gratis, even as Father and Mother Divine do, without salaries, compensation or remuneration for their spiritual work and service.

2

We believe in full employment for all able-bodied persons. No true Follower of Father Divine is on relief.

a

Social Security and Compulsory Insurance are not only unconstitutional but unnecessary when men express their individual independence as true Americans.

3

We pay our way as we go, cash on the spot and refuse to purchase on credit or on the installment plan.

4

We believe in mass production as the best means of eliminating poverty and want universally.

5

We believe that all men have the right to be safe and secure in any possession permitted under the Constitution.

Religiously

1

We believe that the Scripture is being fulfilled as recorded in the King James Version of the Old and New Testaments of the Holy Bible.

2

We believe that Father Divine fulfills the Scriptural Prophecy of the Second Coming of Christ for the Christian world and the Coming of the Messiah for the Jewish world.

3

We have One Father and One Mother—God—Personified in Father Divine and His Spotless Virgin Bride—Mother Divine.

a

Therefore, we are One Family Indivisible; for humanity can only be brothers when there is *One* Father and *One* Mother. We live in the Brotherhood of man under the Fatherhood of God.

4

We believe that the Principles of all true religion are synonymous.

a

True religion is faith in One Indivisible God.

b

Therefore, we live the Ten Commandments and especially according to the precepts given in Jesus' Sermon on the Mount.

5

We believe that Heaven is a State of Consciousness which is being materialized and shall be universally established in fulfillment of Jesus' prayer: "Let Thy Kingdom come and Thy Will be done on earth. . . ."

a

We believe that America is the Birth Place of the Kingdom of God on earth and It shall be fully realized when all men live the synonymous Principles of true Americanism, Brotherhood, Democracy, Christianity, Judaism and all true religion.

6

We believe that Woodmont fulfills the prophecy of the Mount of the House of the Lord from which shall go forth the Law to all nations, spoken of in Isaiah 2:2,3 and Micah 4:1,2.

a

The Woodmont Estate is owned by The Palace Mission, Inc., which maintains it as Father and Mother Divine's private residence. It is only open to the public on Father's and Mother's personal invitation.

7

Under the Peace Mission Movement, there are five incorporated Churches with branches in the U.S.A. and throughout the world.

a
The church services are without ritual and the general public is welcome to attend and participate harmoniously.
b
We believe in the serving of Communion daily after the manner of the Lord's Supper, as practical service for the sustenance of the bodies and benefit of the soul.
c
Those of other faiths may participate in the Holy Communion Service if they wish to do so, partaking of the material food simply as sustenance for their physical bodies.

8
We do not proselyte, because The Life of Christ, when lived is magnetic.
a
Messages and Sermons given by Father and Mother Divine can be obtained from the New Day Publishing Co., 1600 W. Oxford Street, Philadelphia, Pa., 19121.

Thank You, Father and Mother Divine

Appendix B

Songs
of the
Movement

The Peace Mission literally sings itself along. Dozens of songs are sung, many for the first time, at every service. No one is too young or too old to initiate a song at any time during the worship. Rarely is a song brought in from the "world"—most are original; there are no old-time hymns or spirituals. Only occasionally will the music be familiar; usually it is composed by someone in the Movement. Communion Banquets and Anniversary Celebrations are punctuated with songs sung by the assembled throng, by soloists, or by the Rosebuds, Lily-Buds, or Crusaders as a single choir or as three separate choruses. Music is rehearsed only for performances by the Crusaders, Rosebuds, or Lily-Buds for special ceremonies such as Bible School or Adult School Graduations (each about twice yearly in Philadelphia) or for the yearly Wedding Anniversary or Woodmont Open House and Anniversary.

Some typical songs are given here which have been labeled by this author for the type of message they convey. The greatest number in our collection have love for Father-Mother Divine as their theme, and the second largest number express thanks for release from insecurity due to material lacks or social discrimination. The third largest category is declaration of faith in the objectives of the Movement including statements of those objectives. These are labeled as social justice.

A number are statements of followers' creeds and beliefs put into song.

The music is so lively and rhythmical, although not exactly jazz, that one feels that one must join the foot tapping, clapping, and dancing which often accompanies the songs. The dancing is mostly by women and is entirely individualistic and unrehearsed. No one style or step prevails and it is apt to occur at the dancer's seat or in the aisle or even up on the stage in front of the auditorium or hall. Dancing can start up at any time, but usually when the music ceases the dancers sit down and they never interrupt Bible reading or reading from the *New Day*. Anywhere from one to thirty people may be whirling and gliding in as many different ways at any one time. Never have two people been seen dancing together, nor more than two men dancing at one time. Men and women never dance close to each other. Men are seated separately from women and they dance at their seat or in the aisle immediately adjacent to it. Only once did one very old gentleman dance his way toward the front of the audience. Otherwise women dominate the dancing and the space.

Songs of Love

Crusaders' Songs

All the Things You Are
(to the popular tune of the same name)

Time and again I've longed for adventure,
Something to make my heart beat the faster,
What did I long for? I never really knew.
Finding YOUR Love I found my adventure,
Seeing YOUR Smile my heart beats the faster,
All that I want in all of this world is YOU, Dear FATHER!

(chorus)

YOU are the Promised One of Heaven
For Whom the world has waited so long!
YOU are the breathless hush of ev'ning
That trembles on the brink of a lovely song.
YOU are the angel glow
That lights a star,
The dearest things I know
Are what YOU are!
This day my happy heart enfolds YOU,
This day I know GOD's glory Divine
For all the things YOU are, are mine!

God in a Body

I look before me and I see
GOD in a Body so tender and sweet,
HIS Love's for you, HIS Love's for me,
This is the Love that will set you free!
When you realize and consider
And stop and think and figure,

Who is this with so much Love?
Where does it come from?
Where does it go?
I'll tell you one thing for I know
That this is the great Love Master HIMSELF!
Now look before you and you'll see
GOD in a Body so tender and sweet
HIS Love's for you, HIS Love's for me,
This is Love that will set you free!

Honestly

Honestly, I love YOU
I love You with all this heart,
When skies are blue or grey
I'll always feel this way,
Forever and a day I love You so!
Honestly, I love YOU,
I loved YOU right from the start
and my Dearest FATHER
I'll prove it's true somehow,
I love you, I do, honestly!

To Love You

I want to love YOU, FATHER,
A little bit more each day,
I want to love YOU, FATHER,
In all I do and say,
I want to love YOU, FATHER
For the wondrous Works YOU do,
For I know YOU're GOD ALMIGHTY
AND I've given this heart to YOU!

I want to love YOU, FATHER,
When I wake up in the morning,
Love YOU, FATHER,
Every moment of the day,
And when I lay me down to sleep
This prayer I'll say to YOU, my Sweet,
Teach me to love YOU, FATHER,
A little bit more, a little bit more
A little bit more each day!

Dear Father, We're Persuaded

Dear FATHER, we're persuaded
That YOUR Chaste Love
Has drawn our hearts in YOU, Dear,
And they're dissolved.
Each heart-throb pulsates in YOU,
in YOU alone,
United with YOUR Own Heart Beat,
in Holy Song!
And Dear, we are persuaded
That there's no power
That exists or can be created
To put us asunder,
For we are One with YOU, Dear,
In every way,
In all we do and say, Eternally!

Father, I Will Love You Always

FATHER, I will love YOU always,
YOU fill our hearts with joy and with praise,
YOUR Love to me means everything,
Such happiness only YOU can bring,
Life is now forever ideal,
Everybody knows YOU are REAL!
Down in this heart I'll hold YOU tight,
FATHER, I will love YOU always!

You're My Everything

You're the beating of my heart,
You're the twinkling of my eye,
YOU're the joy when I'm living,
YOU're the sunshine of my smile,
YOU're the rainbow when it rains,
YOU're the music when I sing,
YOU're the love in my love songs,
Darling, YOU're my EVERYTHING!
YOU're the beauty of winter,
YOU're the tenderness of spring,
YOU're the romance of summer,
Darling, YOU're my EVERYTHING!

YOU're the keeper of my heart,
YOU're the little birds that sing,
YOU're the true blue of heaven,
Darling, YOU're my EVERYTHING!

I have found a Loving Sweetheart,
I have found a Loving Friend,
I have found a Darling FATHER,
I have found the Star of Stars!
I have found a Smiling Rose,
I have found the Dearest One,
I have found a Diamond clear,
I have found a Friend so Dear,
I have found FATHER DIVINE!

Sweetheart of my soul I love YOU,
YOU're the springtime in my heart,
YOU're the Light by day and night,
YOU are GOD, FATHER DIVINE!
I have found a Loving Sweetheart,
I have found a Loving Friend,
I have found the Star of Stars,
I have found a Smiling Rose,
I have found my Dearest One!

A Lovely Garden

Flowers may bloom in the springtime.
Flowers may bloom in the summer
But the Flower that blooms
Year in and year out
Is the Rose of my heart,
'Tis YOU, sweet FATHER!
Nowhere you can find such a fragrance
As in YOUR Garden of Love
Where Christ alone reigns supreme
On the throne of each Rosebud's heart!

(chorus)

I know a lovely Garden
Where blooms the sweetest
Of all flowers,

Here you will find joy and peace of mind,
Complete happiness eternally!
Yes, I know a lovely Garden
Where blooms the sweetest
Of all flowers,
Here you will find FATHER and MOTHER DIVINE,
King and Queen of Virginity!

Thanks for Personal Welfare

Rosebuds' Songs

Happiness

You brought us Happiness
When YOU brought YOUR Body,
Real Happiness lies in YOUR Holy Body!
YOU paid for this precious gem of life
With YOUR Personal Sacrifice,
   Now we enjoy—real Happiness
That centuries men have searched for,
Happiness, and FATHER Darling, what's more,
We're so blessed to be partakers of
YOUR Holy untouched Love
And Perfect Happiness!

Father's Love

It's FATHER's Love that makes the world go round,
It's FATHER's Love that makes the world go round,
Carry HIS Love in your heart
You and HE will never part,
It's FATHER's Love that makes the world go round.
Oh Hallelujah, can't you see
YOU'll live throughout eternity,
Health and happiness will be your only friend
Till mortality be gone.
Fill your heart with GOD'S Sweet Song.
YOU'll be triumphant and victorious in the end!

Crusaders' Songs

We Don't Have to Die
(to the tune of "Tiptoe Through the Tulips")

Now we have a FATHER
Now we have a MOTHER
Real dear and true Holy Parents.
FATHER gives us wisdom
And HE leads us onward
Into Eternal Life,
That's why we are——

(chorus)

So glad we don't have to
Die to travel
At the light-rate speed
To reach GOD
So far up in the sky!
We're so glad we don't have to
Die to travel at the light-rate speed
To reach GOD so far up in the sky!
We know that FATHER is HERE,
HE's wiped our tears away;
That's why we are so glad
We don't have to
Die to travel
At the light-rate speed
To reach GOD
So far up in the sky!

Take All You Want But Don't Forget the Best!

FATHER has taught us the mystery
Of Happiness and Health,
HE has given us the Abundance
Of Prosperity and Wealth,
HE said, "Take all you want
But don't forget the Best,
For if you do you will lose all the rest!"
We love YOU, FATHER, we will never forget!

We love YOU, FATHER, we know YOU are the
   BEST!

FATHER, we appreciate the Abundance
That YOU give,
We love the Holy Life
YOU have taught us to live,
But most of all we love
YOUR Beautiful Body, Dear,
and love YOU for bringing
Our Precious MOTHER here!
We love YOU, FATHER, we will never forget!
We love YOU, FATHER, we know YOU are the
   BEST!

Songs of Social Justice

Perfect Love

FATHER DIVINE AND MOTHER DIVINE
Have lifted a Standard for all Mankind.
From our Dear FATHER flows love and grace,
We see by HIS Grace the light of HIS Face
Lifting us from all human affection,
From all those ties that lead to destruction.
GOD gave this freedom that works salvation,
Now we can revel for we're free.
Yes, we are all so free indeed!

(chorus)

FATHER, this day we give our hearts
ALL to YOU!
MOTHER, this day we know Your Love
Is so true!
Love, love Holy Love, Pure love,
For which the world is seeking
And Praying.
Oh, Perfect Love!
GOD, GOD, we love YOU, only
Dear GOD our LORD!

Crusaders' Songs

I Believe
(Inspiration came through a Rosebud. Song taken fron The Crusaders'
Declaration Concerning GOD.)

I believe, in the Sacred, Holy
Spiritual Marriage of FATHER DIVINE,
Who is our FATHER, MOTHER GOD,
To HIS Spotless Virgin Bride, MOTHER DIVINE.
Who before the world was, was predestined to be
And now is the Symbol of the Church
Without spot or wrinkle!
I believe that the Marriage of FATHER DIVINE
To MOTHER DIVINE was predestined to be,
That it is the Marriage of the LAMB and the
   BRIDE
And that it symbolizes the Marriage
Of CHRIST to the Church,
The union of GOD and man
And the fusion of Heaven and earth,
I believe! I believe!

(repeat from beginning)
(bass solo) Oh, I believe
(tenor solo) Yes, I believe.

Appendix C

Businesses Conducted by Followers (1938, 1942, 1956, 1961, 1978)

The newspaper of the Movement is sacred to the followers and, therefore, it is assumed that they have always supported it in every way, including helping to finance it by inserting advertisements for their businesses. On this assumption a count of the businesses represented by advertisements is used as an index of the entrepreneurial activities of the members of the Movement. Although there are insertions from nonmembers as well as members, the ads of the latter category are marked by religious names, such as Blessed Peace or Peace Restaurant. The issues selected for analysis were special issues commemorating some event, which therefore carried more advertising than a regular weekly issue. Thus, it is more likely that all followers would have advertised in them in order to support their more costly production.

In the April 14, 1938, issue of the *New Day,* the following businesses advertised:

Restaurants, 7 (1 in New York City [all New York references are to New York City unless otherwise indicated], 1 in Brooklyn, 5 in New Jersey) "Featuring Father's Prices 10 and 15 cents."
Grocers, 1 (Newark, N.J.)
Fish Market, 1 (Newark)
Men's Furnishings, 3 (2 in New York, 1 in Newark)
Ladies' Wear, 2 (New York)
Laundries, 4 (New York)
Shoe Repairing, 2 (New York)
Music Lessons, 1 (New York)
Auto Repairing, 1 (New York)
Manufacturing, 1 Electric Bed Warmer (Denver, Colo.)
Shoe Shining, 2 (New York)
Watchmaking, 1 (New York)

In the September 17, 1942, *New Day*:

Restaurants, 12 (4 in Philadelphia, 1 in New Rochelle, 2 in New York, 5 in New
  Jersey)
Grocers, 4 (3 in New York, 1 in New Jersey)
Fish Markets, 3 (2 in New York,1 in Philadelphia)
Fruits and Vegetables, 3 (2 in New York, 1 in Philadelphia)
Meat Market, 1 (New York)
Men's Furnishings, 1 (New Jersey)
Ladies' Wear, 2 (Philadelphia)
Laundries, 1 (New York)
Shoe Repairing, 5 (New York)
Music Lessons, 0
Auto Repairing, 1 (New York)
Shoe Shining, 7 (New York)
Manufacturing, 0
Watchmaking, 1 (New York)

The following were new categories in 1942, which did not appear in 1938:

Paper Hanger, 1 (New York)
Express Trucking, 7 (New York)
Tire Shop, 1 (New York)
Tailors, 2 (New York)
Jeweler, 1 (New York)
Woodyard, 1 (New York)
Dry Cleaning, 1 (New York)
Ice and Coal, 3 (New York)
Battery Service, 1 (New York)
Radio Repair, 1 (New York)
Barber Shop, 1 (New York)
Thrift Shop, 1 (New York)
Hat Store, 1 (New York)
Carpenter, 1 (New York)

There were altogether 64 advertisers in 1942, of which all but 16 were in New
York City. Eight were in Philadelphia.

In 1938 there were 26, of which 16 were in New York City, 1 in Brooklyn, 8 in
New Jersey, 1 in Denver, Colorado, and none in Philadelphia.

Between 1938 and 1942 38 businesses and several new categories of activities had
been added. However, most of the businesses were in different localities and
under different management than at the earlier date. This would seem to indicate
a high rate of exodus from business or from the Movement.

We may note that, despite the fact that Father Divine had moved his headquarters to Philadelphia in July 1942, new businesses had not yet sprung up there. It is not possible to tell exactly what war pressure did to the businesses. Wartime food shortages may have closed some of the restaurants.

A special issue of the *New Day* appeared on September 15, 1956. Its 200 pages indicated that there was pressure for all true believers to support it; therefore, we can assume again that anyone in business would avail himself of its pages. This should give us a picture of the survivals of war and prosperity.

Businesses advertising in September 15, 1956, issue of the *New Day*:

Restaurants, 3 (Newark, N.J.)
Markets, 5 (3 Newark, 1 Philadelphia, 1 New York)
Shoe Repairing, 1 (Philadelphia)
Shoe Shining, 1 (Philadelphia)
Paper Hanger, 1 (Philadelphia)
Express Trucking, 4 (New York)
Tailor, 2 (New York)
Jeweler, 1 (New York)
Wood, Kerosene, Coal, Ice, 3 (2 Philadelphia, 1 New York)
Barber Shop, 2 (1 New York, 1 Philadelphia)
Thrift Shop, 1 (Philadelphia)
Lingerie, 1 (Newark)
Dress Shop, Sewing, 2 (1 Newark, 1 Brooklyn)
Landscaping Service, 1 (Philadelphia)
Appliances and Furniture, 1 (San Francisco)
Watchmaking, 1 (New York)

This makes a total of 30 advertisements, only 4 more than in 1938. Only one, the watchmaker, is the same proprietor in the same location. There has been a movement away from New York to Newark and Philadelphia.

Businesses advertised in special issue of the *New Day*, September 16, 1961:

Restaurants, 0 (although there were at least 4 in Philadelpia and some in Newark
    and New York City)
Grocers, 1 (Newark) (there were 2 in Philadelphia)
Clothing, 1 (New York)
Ladies' Dresses, 2 (1 in Newark, 1 in Oakland, Calif.)
Novelty Shop, 1 (New York)
Electrical Contractor, 1 (Newark)
Hat Store, 1 (New York)

Watchmaker, 1 (New York) (the only continuous advertiser since 1938)
Barber, 1 (New York)

Although this was a special issue of the paper with a great many advertisements, these 9 businesses were the only ones run by followers of the Movement that advertised. The author knows of two groceries, a barber shop, a dress shop, and two restaurants in Philadelphia, run by followers, that were not included. But even these would bring the total up to only 15 in 1962, which is 11 less than advertised in 1938 and 49 less than advertised in 1942. There had apparently been a large drop in the members conducting their own small businesses. Those businesses which are left may be larger and more profitable than the earlier ones. There is no way to ascertain this.

By 1978 many followers were retired, many were "co-workers," working full time in church activities, and others were at work in a variety of positions in the larger society.

Appendix D

Properties
of the
Peace Mission
Movement (1956)

For the annual celebration of the dedication of Woodmont, an estate on the Main Line at Lower Merion, a suburb of Philadelphia, the Movement usually publishes a special issue of the *New Day*. The 1956 issue contained 200 pages including photographs and descriptions of all the properties owned by the followers in the eastern part of the United States.

The following description indicates the attitudes held toward physical property better than any summary of mine would do. They are given here just as printed in the September 15, 1956, issue of the *New Day*. Each was the caption of a full-page picture of the property. Most of them are still in use in 1978.

The introductory statement reads, "The following are photos of some of the properties in north-eastern United States, acquired by Followers of FATHER DIVINE, owned and operated by them—governed by HIS mind, spirit and Teachings."

FATHER DIVINE SAYVILLE HOME, 72 Macon Street, Sayville, Long Island.

> FATHER and MOTHER moved out here in 1919. It was here to this beautiful country HOME that thousands flocked, hungry in body, spirit and mind. They came from the far corners of the earth to hear the words of wisdom that fell from the lips of FATHER DIVINE and to witness the miraculous healings and blessings of every description wrought by FATHER DIVINE upon those who trod this Holy Ground and believed. It was here that HIS Welcome Table first came into manifestation in that vicinity for the masses to freely come and dine, absolutely gratis. It was here that humanity universally began to realize the priceless gift of the return of OUR SAVIOR here on earth.

Nazareth Mission Church, Home and Training School, Inc., of Pennsylvania, 1600–1614 West Oxford Street, Philadelphia, Pa., FATHER DIVINE, Pastor.

This beautiful structure, with its large auditorium and Holy Communion Banquet Hall, is located at the corner of Oxford and 16th Streets, Philadelphia, the Cradle of Democracy. It stands as a church, home and training school in serving and aiding the people; not only as a haven of peace and good will for the mind and spirit, but also as a benefactor in reaching those needing aid materially and physically. This service is rendered not just one day in the year, but each day in the year, without regard to so-called race, creed or color, in the true spirit and life of the lowly Nazarene.

Palace Mission Church and Home, Inc., of New Jersey, 22 Halleck Street, Newark, N.J., Rev. M. J. Divine, Ms. D., D.D., Pastor.

The Palace Mission Church . . . acquired this large piece of property at 22 Halleck Street in the residential district of Newark, N.J.—the land itself being approximately 235 ft. by 142 ft. by 96 ft. in size, fronts both Halleck Street and the main street at the rear of the property. This is the large 3-story brick, stone and concrete building on the premises which has been renovated. There is an auditorium and Holy Communion Banquet Room. Because of the large windows all the rooms are bright and cheerful.

Palace Mission Church and Home, Inc., The Home for the Aged and Nurses' Training School, Central Avenue at Tenth St., Newark, N.J., Father Divine, Pastor.

A modern fireproof, brick, 4-story, 87-room Hospital building with elevator service. It is situated on the corner of Central Avenue and 19th Street in Newark, New Jersey. Transportation facilities to the center of town are available.

Unity Mission Church, Home and Training School, Inc., of New York, 103 West 117th St., New York City, Father Divine, Pastor.

In the heart of upper New York City, affords dormitory accommodations as well as a large Holy Communion Banquet Room. There is also a spacious public meeting hall to which many come and gather in the Unity of spirit, mind, aim and purpose in bearing witness and giving praise and thanksgiving to FATHER DIVINE for HIS wondrous works to and for all mankind.

Peace Center and Nazareth Missions' Home for the Aged, Church and Training School, Inc., of New York, 13–17 W. 128th St., New York City.

This substantial five-story building on property that extends over to 129th St., has every modern convenience. It contains a fully equipped school, library, chapel, music room, social center, and community rooms, Holy Communion Banquet Hall, kitchens, offices and sleeping accommodations with baths and showers. This . . . was purchased by two of the churches of the Peace Mission Movement. A large building housing the brothers' quarters is located directly behind this building.

Circle Mission Church, Home and Training School, Inc., 764–772 Broad Street, Philadelphia, Father Divine, Pastor.

Located in Philadelphia, the "City of Brotherly Love" and "The Country Seat of the World," is the Headquarters of FATHER DIVINE. It stands as a light to and for the service of all mankind. Here is put into actuality, the Golden Rule, Brotherhood, Democracy, Americanism and Christianity, and as it is here so it is becoming to be from land to land and from shore to shore. (Bought in 1939 for $50,000.)

Unity Mission Church, Home and Training School, Inc., of Pennsylvania, 907 N. 49th Street, Philadelphia, Pa.

This beautiful structure, the Unity Mission Church . . . has two branch churches in Philadelphia. As a sample and example of practical Christianity, Brotherhood and Americanism this church stands, meeting the needs of the people and especially those in the immediate vicinity, as a haven of Peace and good will to all. Its schoolrooms with free educational facilities, large auditorium gymnasium, bowling alleys, music room, playground and beautiful Holy Communion Private Dining Room are tangible evidence of the blessings of God on earth to and for the good of all mankind.

United Mission Church, Home and Training School and Bible Institute, Inc., of Philadelphia, 1530 N. 16th Street, Philadelphia, Pa., Father Divine, Pastor.

This beautiful building . . . is also a branch of the Unity Mission . . . at 907 N. 41st Street, Philadelphia. Here Bible classes are held for all desiring to attend. A large auditorium classroom and a beautiful, spacious Holy Communion Dining Room are maintained as well as a Rectory for the Dean. Truly, FATHER DIVINE has raised up a standard of perfection of Righteousness, Honesty, Virtue and Holiness in this land and established a House of Prayer for all the people.

Unity Mission Church, Home and Training School Annex, Inc., 511–17 South 21st St., Philadelphia, Pa., Father Divine, Pastor.

A branch of the Unity Mission . . . 907 North 41st St. This building . . . is a blessing to those in the immediate vicinity, especially for the youth of the neighborhood. Here a clean and wholesome atmosphere predominates . . . also has a large auditorium.

Circle Mission Church, Home and Training School, Inc., 2064 Boston Road, Bronx, New York, Father Divine, Pastor.

This beautiful edifice . . . is a model home for the aged, church, chapel and community center.

Parsonage of Palace Mission Church, Home and Training School, Inc., of New York, 305 W. 107th Street, New York City, Father Divine, Pastor.

Near Riverside Drive and from its front windows can be seen the Hudson River. With its many spacious rooms it is dedicated to the service of humanity and set apart as a parsonage for the Pastor, Father Divine.

Former Residence and Parsonage, 1887–89 Madison Avenue, New York City.

This beautiful building, the former New York City residence of FATHER DIVINE before HE established HIS present residence of Philadelphia is . . . situated directly opposite one of the city's many beautiful public parks and playgrounds. Of the more than 50 rooms in this edifice, comprising offices, private suite for Father Divine . . . Mother Divine and HIS staff, tea room, living room, and sleeping accommodations, there is also a large Holy Communion Banquet Hall. It still remains a Parsonage for many of the ministers under the Peace Mission Movement.

Mansions

Yonkers Mansion, 369 Park Hill Ave., Yonkers, Westchester County, New York.

This beautiful home . . . owned by followers of FATHER DIVINE and operated under HIS Mind and Spirit, is located in the exclusive Park Hill residential district. Set in a pattern of greenery, the house is surrounded by tall trees and many flower beds. On the property consisting of over an acre and a half of ground, is also a large greenhouse. Not far distant is the scenic Saw Mill River Parkway, permitting quick and easy access to New York City as well as a main thoroughfare to upstate New York and Long Island.

Divine Tarrytown Estate, Tarrytown, Westchester County, New York.

In the exclusive residential district of Tarrytown . . . overlooking the Hudson River, stands this beautiful 70-acre estate, assessed at nearly three-quarters of a million dollars, owned by a few followers of FATHER DIVINE. From the windows of the residence set high on a hill, one can catch an inspiring view of the countryside for miles around. This lovely stone mansion surrounded with gorgeous shrubbery and trees, is so constructed as to withstand the severest winters. In the springtime, countless varieties of brilliant flowers and foliage make its rolling landscape a scene of colorful beauty. A private road winds around the property joining the house and the adjacent buildings with the Albany Post Road. (Cost $36,000 in 1940.)

Woodmont, of the Palace Mission, Inc., of New York, Lower Merion, Pennsylvania.

73-acre estate, 32-room mansion, swimming pool. (Bought in 1953 for $75,000 cash; real estate dealers say work done on it to rehabilitate it is worth a quarter million.)

Woodmont—The Mount of the House of the LORD!

Owned by Palace Mission, Inc., and dedicated as the Country Estate of FATHER AND MOTHER DIVINE, September 10, 11, 12, 1953 A.D.F.D.

This imposing thirty-room castle-like mansion built in 1892 at an estimated cost of one million dollars is a French Gothic design and is a steel structure built on solid rock. It is situated on the highest point in Montgomery County at an elevation of 475 ft., overlooking the bend in the Schuylkill River and commanding a view for fifteen miles around. There are 73 acres of picturesque grounds with a tennis court and a 25 x 55 ft. outdoor filtered swimming pool.

Appendix E

Properties of Father Divine's Followers (1962* and 1978†)

New York City "Churches" (These also furnish living quarters and restaurants for their members within the same building)

Unity Mission Church, Home and Training School, Inc., of New York, 103 West 117th St.

Peace Center and Nazareth Missions' Home for the Aged, Church and Training School, Inc., 13–17 West 128th St.

Circle Mission Church, Home and Training School, Inc., 2064 Boston Road, Bronx, N.Y.

New York City Properties (used for residential purposes).

Parsonage of Palace Mission Church, Home and Training School, 305 West 107th St.

Apartment House, 226 West 122nd St.

Brothers' Quarters, Peace Center and Nazareth Missions' Home and Church, 12 West 129th St.

Father Divine's former residence and parsonage, 1887–1889 Madison Ave.

Father Divine Peace Mission Movement Extension, 70 Lefferts Place, Brooklyn.

New York State Properties

Father Divine Sayville Home, 72 Macon Street, Sayville, Long Island.

Divine Tarrytown Estate, Tarrytown, Westchester County (70 acres).

Yonkers Mansion, 369 Park Hill Ave., Yonkers, Westchester County.

Divine Hotel, Krum Elbow Estate, Highland, Ulster County.†

Several Houses on Krum Elbow Estate.*

Divine Hope Farm, West Saugerties, Ulster County (45 acres).†

Father Divine Peace Mission, 67 Chapel St., Kingston, Ulster County.

Divine Farm, Saxton, West Saugerties, Ulster County.†

---

* Some have been sold, but most are still owned in 1978.

† No longer identified with the Movement, 1978.

Philadelphia Churches

Circle Mission Church, Home and Training School, Inc., 764–772 Broad St.

Nazareth Mission Church, Home and Training School, Inc., of Pennsylvania, 1600–1614 West Oxford St.

Unity Mission Church, Home and Training School, Inc., of Pennsylvania, 907 North 41st St.

Unity Mission Church, Home and Training School and Bible Institute, Inc., of Philadelphia, 1530 North 16th St. (Branch of 41st St.)

Unity Mission Church, Home and Training School Annex, Inc., 511–17 South 21st St. (Branch of 41st St.)

Philadelphia Apartments and Residential

Peace Mission Home, 4112 Ogden St.

Divine Lorraine Hotel, Broad St. and Fairmont Ave. (300 rooms, cost $485,000).

Divine Tracy Hotel, 36th and Chestnut Sts. (cost $200,000).

The Divine International House of Palace Mission, Inc., 1430 North Broad St.

Unity Mission Church Apartments, Westminster Ave. and 41st St.

Unity Mission Fraternity Apartments, 892–896 North 41st St.

Unity Mission Apartments and Peace Grocery, 900 North 41st St.

Sorority Peace Mission Evangelical Home, 869 N. 40th St.

Junior Sorority Peace Mission Evangelical Rosebuds' Home, 920–922 N. 19th St.

Fraternity Peace Mission Evangelical Home, 507 S. Broad St.

True American Peace Mission Evangelical Hotel, 2052–2054 Catherine St.

Junior Sorority Rosebuds' Rest, 751 South 19th St. (Has a Peace Grocery Store on ground floor.)

Fraternity Peace Mission Evangelical Hotel Poplar, 1618–1620 Poplar St.

Sorority Home, 1609 Allegheny Avenue.

Evangelical Fraternity Peace Mission Interracial Apartments, 1745 W. Diamond St.

Divine International Peace Mission Evangelical Hotel and Garage, 1802–1808 Ridge Ave.

Philadelphia—Garages

Peace Unity Cooperative Garage, Poplar and Ireland Sts.

Peace Mission Democratic Cooperative Garage, 510–528 South Eighth St.

Suburban Philadelphia—Estate

Woodmont, Woodmont Park of the Palace Mission, Inc., of New York, Spring Mill and Woodmont Roads, Lower Merion, Pennsylvania.

There are also a number of businesses, grocery stores, barber shops, dress shops, restaurants, tailor and cleaning shops, and others housed in the properties listed above and owned and operated by members of the churches.

A fleet of automobiles, mostly Cadillacs, running into a score or more, furnish a transportation system for followers and attenders among the network of churches, homes, and training schools in New York, Philadelphia, New Jersey, extending perhaps at times to Washington, D.C., and Connecticut. This is a major business activity in itself.

Newark, New Jersey, Churches

Palace Mission Church and Home, Inc., The Home for the Aged and Nurses' Training School, Central Ave. at 10th St.
Palace Mission Church and Home, Inc., of New Jersey, 22 Halleck St.

Newark, New Jersey, Hotels and Apartments

Divine Hotel Riviera, Clinton Ave. and High St. (275 rooms, cost $450,000).
Sorority Peace Mission Democratic Apartment House, 125 Spruce St.
Sorority Home, 741–743 High St.
Sorority Evangelical Twin Apartment House, 34–36 Sterling St.

Pine Brook, New Jersey

Palace Mission Church and Home, Inc.,† of Pine Brook, N.J. (formerly the Belmont Country Club and the Sunrise Hotel with 100 rooms and 70 acres of land).

Jersey City, New Jersey

Hotel Fairmount, 2595 Hudson Blvd., Jersey City, N.J. (purchased for $400,000 cash to replace properties in Newark taken over by the Housing Redevelopment and Renewal Program in that area. Belongs to two nonprofit corporations, the Peace Center Church and Home, Inc., and the Palace Mission, Inc. Announced in the *New Day*, February 17, 1962. Has 170 rooms).

California

Circle Mission Church, 964 E. Jefferson Blvd., Los Angeles.
Circle Mission Church, 4061 E. Pacific Ave., Sacramento (1978).

Washington, D.C.

Peace Mission Church.

Chicago, Illinois

Church of the Mary Mystical Rose of Perpetual Hope (affiliated in some way with
the Peace Mission through continuous visits of its pastor and certain members to Philadelphia churches, and the recognition of Father Divine as God
by its members).
4825 Drexel Ave., Chicago, Ill. Services are held there every Sunday at 2:00 P.M.
(advertisement, the *New Day,* October 13, 1962, p. 21).

Republic of Panama

Circle Mission Church, Home and Training School.

Vancouver, British Columbia

Father Divine Peace Mission Extension.

Vienna, Austria

Nazareth Mission Church, Home and Training School, Inc.

Germany

Goettingen, Unity Mission Church, Home and Training School (1978).

Switzerland

Rheineck, Unity Mission Church, Home and Training School.
Wallisellen, Circle Mission Church, Querstrasse 2 (1978).

British Guiana

Campbellville, Demarara

Australia

Elwood, Victoria, Peace Mission.
Drummoyne, Sydney, Nazareth Mission Church, Home and Training School of
Australia.

Most of these properties are documented by photographs of the buildings, of services, and of members in various issues of the *New Day* during 1962, and later.

Notes

Preface

1

Kenneth E. Burnham, "Father Divine: A Case Study of Charismatic Leadership," Ph.D. dissertation, University of Pennsylvania, 1963.

2

For discussion, see H. T. Dohrman, *California Cult* (Boston: Beacon Press, 1958), pp. 139–142; Bryan R. Wilson, *Sects and Society* (Berkeley: University of California Press, 1961), p. 7; Leon Festinger, Henry Riecken, and Stanley Schachter, *When Prophecy Fails* (Minneapolis: University of Minnesota Press, 1956), pp. 237–252; and Solomon Poll, "The Economic Organization of a Religious Community," Ph.D. dissertation, University of Pennsylvania, 1961, pp. 353–369.

3

Neil J. Smelser, *Theory of Collective Behavior* (New York: Free Press, 1963), pp. 348–349.

4

Hadley Cantril, *The Psychology of Social Movements* (New York: Wiley, 1944), ch. 5; Wendell C. King, *Social Movements in the United States* (New York: Random House, 1950).

5

Although the church–sect contrast was introduced by Ernst Troeltsch, *The Social Teaching of the Christian Churches*, vol. 1, trans. Olive Wyon (New York: Macmillan, 1931), has been modified, refined, and expanded upon by Howard Becker, Milton Yinger, Peter Berger, D. A. Martin, Richard Niebuhr, and others, it is still being "worked over." For one of the later attempts and extensive bibliography, cf. Benton Johnson, "On Church and Sect," *American Sociological Review* 28 (August): 539–549, 1963.

6

Bryan R. Wilson, *Sects and Society*, pp. 325–354. Cf. also Allan W. Eister, *Drawing Room Conversion: A Sociological Account of the Oxford Group Movement* (Durham: Duke University Press, 1950), ch. 3.

I   From Reverend to Father

1

Some of his followers disapprove of using the word *man* to refer to Major Jealous Divine, but he himself did; for example: "I came to establish the Kingdom on earth among men, but I came as a man to men . . . I came to those who were living an illegal life that I might show them how not to live according to the flesh!" Spoken June 21, 1933; reprinted in *New Day*, May 18, 1968, p. 10.

2

Wendell C. King, *Social Movements in the United States* (New York: Random House, 1950), p. 36.

3

Charles Y. Glock, "The Sociology of Religion," in *Sociology Today*, ed. Robert K. Merton

(New York: Basic Books, 1959), p. 163.
4
Max Weber, *The Theory of Social and Economic Organization*, trans. A. M. Henderson and Talcott Parsons (New York: Oxford University Press, 1947), p. 359.
5
Anthony F. C. Wallace, "Revitalization Movements," *American Anthropologist* 58 (April): 274, 1956.
6
Max Weber, *From Max Weber: Essays in Sociology*, trans. H. H. Gerth and C. Wright Mills (New York: Oxford University Press, 1958), p. 295. All quotations from Weber in this discussion will refer to this volume, pp. 294 ff.
7
Pauline V. Young, *The Pilgrims of Russian Town* (Chicago: University of Chicago Press, 1932); H. H. Stroup, *Jehovah's Witnesses* (New York: Columbia University Press, 1945); Arthur H. Fauset, *Black Gods of the Metropolis* (Philadelphia: University of Pennsylvania Press, 1944); A. W. Eister, *Drawing Room Conversion* (Durham: Duke University Press, 1950); Thomas O'Dea, *The Mormons* (Chicago: University of Chicago Press, 1957); Bryan R. Wilson, *Sects and Society* (Berkeley: University of California Press, 1961); C. R. Whitley, *Trumpet Call of Reformation* (St. Louis: Bethany Press, 1959); H. T. Dohrman, *California Cult* (Boston: Beacon Press, 1958); John A. Hostetler, *Amish Society* (Baltimore: Johns Hopkins University Press, 1963); Solomon Poll, *The Hasidic Community of Williamsburg* (Glencoe, Ill.: Free Press, 1962); Howard Brotz, *The Black Jews of Harlem* (Glencoe, Ill.: Free Press, 1964); John Lofland, *Doomsday Cult* (Englewood Cliffs, N.J.: Prentice-Hall, 1966); C. Eric Lincoln, *The Black Muslims in America* (Boston: Beacon Press, 1961); B. H. Garner, *Indian Shakers: A Messianic Cult of the Pacific Northwest* (Carbondale: Southern Illinois University Press, 1957); J. A. Beckford, *The Trumpet of Prophecy: A Sociological Study of Jehovah's Witnesses* (New York: Wiley, 1975); Leonard Barrett, *The Rastafarians* (Boston: Beacon Press, 1977); E. T. Clark, *The Small Sects in America* (Nashville: Abingdon Press, 1949); Norman Cohn, *Pursuit of the Millennium* (New York: Essential Books, 1957); Marley Cole, *Jehovah's Witnesses: The New World Society* (New York: Vantage Press, 1955); James A. Dator, *Soka Gakkai: Builders of the Third Civilization* (Seattle: University of Washington Press, 1969); R. S. Ellwood, *One-Way: The Jesus Movement* (Englewood Cliffs, N.J.: Prentice-Hall, 1972); R. S. Ellwood, *Religious and Spiritual Groups in Modern America* (Englewood Cliffs, N.J.: Prentice-Hall, 1973); C. Y. Glock and R. N. Bellah, eds., *The New Religious Consciousness* (Berkeley: University of California Press, 1976); J. A. Hostetler, *Hutterite Society* (Baltimore: Johns Hopkins University Press, 1974); J. A. Hostetler, *Communitarian Societies* (New York: Holt, Rinehart and Winston, 1974); J. S. Judah, *Hare Krishna and the Counterculture* (New York: Wiley, 1974); W. H. Kephart, *Extraordinary Groups* (New York: St. Martin's Press, 1976); V. Lantenari, *The Religions of the Oppressed* (New York: Knopf, 1963); W. La Barre, *They Shall Take Up Serpents* (Minneapolis: University of Minnesota Press, 1962); J. Needleman, *The New Religions* (New York: Doubleday, 1970); G. K. Nelson, *Spiritualism and Society* (London: Routledge and Kegan Paul, 1969); J. S. Slotkin, *The Peyote Religion* (Glencoe, Ill.: Free Press, 1956); F. Sontag, *Sun Myung Moon* Nashville: Abingdon Press, 1977); R. Wallis, *The Road to Total Freedom* (New York: Columbia University Press, 1977); B. R. Wilson, *Religious Sects* (New York: McGraw-Hill, 1970); B. Zablocki, *The Joyful Community* (Baltimore: Penguin Books, 1971); I. R. Zaretsky and Mark P. Leone, eds., *Religious Movements in Contemporary America* (Princeton, N.J.: Princeton University Press, 1974).
8.
New York News, August 20, 1932, pp. 1-3.

9
Ibid., December 17, 1934.
10
Ibid., December 20, 1934. This newspaper was sympathetic to Father Divine and used the Movement's style of capitalization in quoting him.
11
Weber was much concerned with the problems of power, authority, and domination in both political and religious contexts. Reinhard Bendix has dealt most comprehensively with Weber's work in this area in *Max Weber: An Intellectual Portrait* (Garden City, N.Y.: Doubleday, 1960), pp. 287–459.
12
John Hoshor, *God in a Rolls Royce* (New York: Hillman Curl, 1936); Robert A. Parker, *The Incredible Messiah* (Boston: Little, Brown, 1937); Sara Harris, *Father Divine: Holy Husband* (Garden City, N.Y.: Doubleday, 1953) and *Father Divine*, rev. ed. (New York: Collier, 1971).
13
This statement is reprinted many times in the pages of *New Day* as well as in a manuscript prepared by the Office of Information, Circle Mission Church, Home and Training School, Inc.
14
These are all newspapers, published in various parts of the United States between 1930 and 1936, which were friendly to the Movement. The *New Day*, the followers' weekly newspaper, has been published continuously since 1936. Father Divine did approve of one publication by an outsider: Charles S. Braden, *These Also Believe* (New York: Macmillan, 1949). Also relevant are a study by a psychologist, Hadley Cantril, *The Psychology of Social Movements* (New York: Wiley, 1944), pp. 123–143, and by an anthropologist, Arthur Huff Fauset, *Black Gods of the Metropolis*, pp. 52–67. A Ph.D. dissertation at Boston University was written by Grady Demus Davis: "A Psychological Investigation of Motivational Needs and Their Gratification in the Father Divine Movement," 1953.
15
Letter from the Office of Information, Circle Mission Church, Philadelphia, 1961.
16
The ones that Father Divine names are *The Secret of the Ages, The Secret of Gold, The Life Magnet,* and "all of his books." They were published by Collier himself in New York in the 1920s.
17
An account of a meeting with the "Great Masters of the Himalayas" who helped impart spiritual knowledge to the author (San Francisco: California Press, 1942).
18
Quoted many times in *New Day* and in the manuscript referred to in an earlier note.
19
New Day, August 28, 1954, p. 15. (Spoken in 1942.)

II   Father Divine Recognized as God

1
This letter has been reproduced many times in the Movement's literature. This copy is from *New Day*, April 29, 1956.
2
Eugene Del Mar's name appeared in many issues of *Who's Who in America* in the 1930s. He was a successful businessman, lawyer, stockbroker, and author of several books on religion. He died in the 1940s.

3
New Day, April 28, 1956, pp. 58–59.
4
Ibid., April 22, 1961, p. 18.
5
Ibid., April 29, 1961, p. 11.
6
Ibid., pp. 10–11.
7
Ibid., p. 11.
8
Ibid., October 1, 1942, pp. 65–66.
9
Personal interviews and testimonies in *New Day.*
10
Max Weber, *The Protestant Ethic and the Spirit of Capitalism,* trans. Talcott Parsons (New York: Charles Scribner's Sons, 1958), pp. 108–109.
11
These were the first of more than 300 reports that the *New York Times* has carried since then. *Newsweek* published twelve items from 1933 to 1978; *Time* printed fourteen between 1936 and 1978.
12
Robert Allerton Parker, *The Incredible Messiah: The Deification of Father Divine* (Boston: Little, Brown, 1937), p. 24.
13
New Day, April 18, 1940, occasioned by newspaper criticism of a mission in Stratford, Connecticut.
14
Ibid., April 28, 1956, p. 37.
15
Ibid.
16
Bryan R. Wilson, *Sects and Society,* p. 10.

III   Father Divine Is God

1
Letter-signed "Rev. M. J. Divine, MsD., D.D. (Better known as FATHER DIVINE)" addressed to a correspondent in Africa, October 26, 1961, published in *New Day,* November 11, 1961, p. 14.
2
And, as with all the thousands of letters signed by Father Divine during thirty years of publication, the last paragraph informs the world: "Thus, I desire that you may be as this leaves ME, for I AM, as I shall eternally be, Well, Healthy, Joyful, Peaceful, Lively, Loving, Successful, Prosperous and Happy in Spirit, Body and Mind in every organ, muscle, sinew, joint, limb, vein and bone and even in every ATOM, fibre and cell of MY BODILY FORM." Ibid.
3
Ibid.
4
Ibid.

5
Cf. C. B. Crumb, Jr., "Father Divine's Use of Colloquial and Original English," *American Speech* 15:327, 1940.
6
New Day, November 11, 1961, p. 14.
7
Ibid., p. 12.
8
Ibid.
9
Ibid.
10
Ibid. The punctuation and capitalization of all the quotations from the recorded words of Father Divine are just as the Movement's editors print them.
11
Ibid., September 1, 1938, pp. 22–23.
12
See Max Weber, *The Protestant Ethic and the Spirit of Capitalism,* trans. Talcott Parsons (New York: Charles Scribner's Sons, 1958).
13
Arthur Huff Fauset, *Black Gods of the Metropolis* (Philadelphia: University of Pennsylvania Press, 1944). Ch. 3, "United House of Prayer for All People," described Daddy Grace's church. Newspapers described his bizarre dress and flowing hair.
14
New Day, II, no. 35, September 1, 1938, p. 23.
15
This is a reference to a statement made earlier in the lesson that Jesus had gone to "the other place" (hell) and conquered the devil.
16
New Day, January 13, 1938, pp. 22–23. The whole of this sermon is reprinted as an example of the manner in which Father Divine delivered his messages and to illustrate the progression of thoughts and the logic used in creating the charismatic milieu around his followers.

IV   God in One Person: Challenge and Answer

1
Statements to the writer by present followers, also stated many times in testimonies printed in *New Day* and earlier publications of the Movement.
2
New Day, March 3, 1938, pp. 15–20.
3
Ibid.
4
From this point the account of this episode is given just as it was printed in *New Day* of March 3, 1938, since this version of the affair represents the "definition of the situation" made by the publishers of the paper, accepted by Father Divine, and, hence, learned and acted upon by the followers.

V   Platform of Rights: Overcoming Racial Discrimination

1

Reprinted many times in *New Day*. The whole platform is in the issue of February 17, 1936, pp. 3–11.

2

This reference to a research department may have been relevant in 1936 when it was written but, from 1961 to 1978, reference to any specific local or state candidate was very rare at any meetings attended by the author.

3

No records are available on numbers of schools organized by the Movement nor of individuals encouraged to return to public school. But the value of education for attaining equal opportunities in voting and employment has always been stressed. Teachers who are Movement members are always available to provide learning and some kind of class is always being offered. New York and Philadelphia churches now conduct classes, mostly at night. The latest announcement in *New Day*, for the fall of 1977, offers many courses, including commercial subjects. No fees are charged; teachers donate their services according to their ability and available time. Public schools are supported as the proper place for formal education; children brought up in the Movement go to public schools and some have been sent through college with the encouragement of the churches.

4

The third and last of the planks in the educational section is as follows: "The abolishing of the conventional form of greeting, 'H-e-l-l-o,' from all educational institutions, and substitution of the word 'PEACE.' We also request the cooperation of the telephone companies in this respect, that a generation with PEACE on its lips instead of what war has been said to be, may come into being."

5

This penalty could not be death according to the Peace Movement for Plank 6 of the section on Principles calls for "Abolishment of capital punishment in all states and countries."

6

New Day, February 17, 1938, pp. 10–11.

7

Ibid., p. 11.

8

The publisher of the German edition spent several months in Philadelphia and New York in 1961. He had been a follower for over twenty-five years but had never seen Father Divine before this visit.

9

These include two very old English ladies, said to be former Christian Science practitioners, who came from England shortly after World War II and live in the old Diston mansion —now a Peace Mission Bible school—in Philadelphia; an Australian woman who used to teach English to migrants from Europe while they were on the boat bound for Australia; two young German (or Swiss) Rosebuds who now work as waitresses in a cafeteria of the Movement and at the Communion table of the West Philadelphia church (Unity Mission); a Swiss craftsman who does all types of maintenance work on the estate at Woodmont; and an English or Australian woman who is an officer in one of the churches. The present Mother Divine was a Canadian.

10

New Day, March 10, 1938, p. 13.

11

High Falls was a farm and home in Ulster County, New York, where, from 1936 on, members of the Movement carried on farming.

12
See *Congressional Record,* vol. 83, pt. 1, January 1938, pp. 753, 761, 817, 828, 829, 831–834.
13
Father Divine told about Peninah's desire to "pass" in many messages printed in *New Day* after his remarriage. The present Mrs. Divine is also quoted many times, and the writer has heard her accept this definition of the situation.
14
Quoted from the cover to the Tenth Wedding Anniversary issue supplement to *New Day,* which consists of a well-printed, two-color, 104-page review of the Marriage and the progress of the Movement; published April 28, 1956. A special issue of *New Day* celebrates each Anniversary.
15
Some of the Newark properties were taken over for an urban redevelopment project. With the money received for them, the Movement bought the fifty- or sixty-year-old Hotel Fairmount in Jersey City. It was well received by the press there, which printed editorials supporting the takeover of what had been a segregated hotel.

VI   Overcoming the Depression

1
New Day, March 3, 1938, p. 20.
2
Ibid., September 17, 1942, p. 101.
3
Ibid., March 3, 1938.
4
Ibid., February 20, 1938.
5
See ch. 17, "Business Enterprise," in E. Franklin Frazier, *The Negro in the United States,* rev. ed. (New York: Macmillan, 1957); St. Clair Drake and Horace R. Cayton, *Black Metropolis* (New York: Harcourt, Brace, 1945), chs. 16 and 17; Richard Sterner, *The Negro's Share* (New York: Harper, 1944); Robert C. Weaver, *Negro Labor* (New York: Harcourt, Brace, 1946); Sterling D. Spero and Abram L. Harris, *The Black Worker* (New York: Harper, 1931). Frazier has made a bitter indictment of the lack of concern of the middle-class Negro for the welfare of the "race" in *Black Bourgeoisie* (Glencoe, Ill.: Free Press, 1956).
6
New Day, April 14, 1938, p. 17.
7
Ibid.
8
Ibid., April 21, 1938, p. 29.
9
Ibid., February 22, 1940, pp. 43–44.
10
Further details on the businesses discussed here and the method of identifying them are given in Appendix C.
11
New Day, April 21, 1938, pp. 29–30.
12
Ibid., June 13, 1949.
13
United Peace Mission Nurses, pamphlet, no date, p. 7.

14
Christian Science has faced this same problem. See Charles H. Braden, *Christian Science Today* (Dallas: Southern Methodist University Press, 1958), pp. 260–262.
15
United Peace Mission Nurses, p. 10.
16
An incident in the restaurant conducted at the Circle Mission Church on South Broad Street in Philadelphia illustrates the ideology of "pay as you go" that is so central to the economics of the Movement. The author often ate there while conducting informal interviews with other diners. A number of small children used to appear quite regularly and leave clutching an ice cream cone. One day the author observed to one of the managers of the restaurant that it was pleasant to see the children enjoying their ice cream. Her answer was, "They pay for it. You don't get anything for nothing in this world." They were neighborhood children, but I expect the same would apply for followers' children.
17
New Day, April 21, 1938, p. 32.
18
Ibid., April 21, 1938.
19
Ibid., April 28, 1956, p. 16.

VII   The Organization of the Peace Mission Movement

1
I have brought together here typical quotations from this period. Father spoke many times in Rockland Palace and in many other auditoriums in Harlem, Brooklyn, Newark, Bridgeport, Philadelphia, New Rochelle, and other places around New York City. He appeared somewhere almost daily and sometimes at several places in one day. *Metaphysical News,* June 8, 1932.
2
Light, May 31, 1933, p. 3.
3
New York News, October 1, 1932.
4
Reflector, Los Angeles, November 7, 1934, p. 3.
5
World Echo, January 27, 1934, p. 2.
6
Divine Light, September 1933, p. 5.
7
New York News, March 3, 1934, pp. 1, 6.
8
Spoken Word, April 13, 1935, pp. 4–7.
9
An affadavit sworn to before a notary public, May 25, 1937. Ibid., June 23, 1937, p. 50.
10
Ibid., pp. 54–55.
11
All references to the By-Laws are based on a copy furnished by an officer of one of the churches. Each church uses the same By-Laws.
12

New Day, February 3, 1968, pp. 28–29.
13
Quoted from a pamphlet published by the Movement, no date.

IX Survival and the Problem of Succession

1
Father Divine's quotation originally appeared on February 6, 1960, and was reprinted almost weekly for several years up to September 1965.
2
New Day, Mar 21, 1960, p. 19.
3
Sara Harris, *Father Divine: Holy Husband* (Garden City, N.Y.: Doubleday, 1953); rev. ed., *Father Divine* (New York: Collier, 1971).
4
Charles S. Braden, *These Also Believe* (New York: Macmillan, 1949), p. 77.
5
Leon Festinger, Henry W. Riecken, and Stanley Schacter, *When Prophecy Fails* (Minneapolis: University of Minnesota Press, 1956), pp. 3–5.
6
New Day, May 20, 1967, p. 29.
7
Ibid., May 4, 1968, pp. 12–13.
8
The following material is from the report of the Meeting of the Unity Mission Church of Philadelphia held June 7, 1977, and printed in *New Day,* July 9, 1977, pp. 16–24.
9
The remnants of the Shaker communities in New Hampshire and Maine are fast approaching their second century of existence. See Marguerite F. Melcher, *The Shaker Adventure* (Cleveland: Western Reserve University, 1960) and Edward D. Andrews, *The People Called Shakers* (New York: Oxford University Press, 1953). For the Oneida community, see R. A. Parker, *Yankee Saint: John Humphrey Noyes and the Oneida Community* (New York: Putnam's, 1935) and J. P. Noyes, *My Father's House* (New York: Farrar, 1937).
10
Max Weber, *The Theory of Economic and Social Organization,* trans. A. M. Henderson and Talcott Parsons (New York: Oxford University Press, 1947), pp. 358–370.

X Conclusion

1
Thomas Ford Hoult, *The Sociology of Religion* (New York: Dryden Press, 1958), p. 120.
2
J. Milton Yinger, *Religion, Society and the Individual* (New York: Macmillan, 1957), p. 305. Cf. Neil J. Smelser, *Theory of Collective Behavior* (New York: Free Press, 1963), pp. 355–356, and K. Lang and G. Lang, *Collective Dynamics* (New York: Crowell, 1961), pp. 231–254, 517–523.
3
H. H. Gerth and C. Wright Mills, *From Max Weber: Essays in Sociology* (New York: Oxford University Press, 1958), pp. 245–252.

4

Max Weber, *The Theory of Social and Economic Organization,* trans. A. M. Henderson and Talcott Parsons (New York: Oxford University Press, 1947), p. 71.

5

Wilson D. Wallis, *Messiahs: Their Role in Civilization* (Washington, D.C.: Public Affairs Press, 1943), p. 201. See also Anthony F. C. Wallace, "Revitalization Movements," *American Anthropologist* 58 (April):274, 1956, and Norman Cohn, *The Pursuit of the Millennium,* 2nd ed. (New York: Harper, 1961).

6

Robert K. Merton, *Social Theory and Social Structure,* rev. ed. (Glencoe, Ill.: Free Press, 1957), p. 162.

7

Ibid., p. 191.

8

Weber, *Theory of Social and Economic Organization,* p. 71.

9

Arnold Rose, *The Negro in America* (condensation of Gunnar Myrdal, *An American Dilemma*) (Boston: Beacon Press, 1944), pp. 1-2.

10

Ibid., pp. 33, 132.

11

Frank Loescher, *The Protestant Church and the Negro* (New York: Association Press, 1948).

12

See the discussion of major American values in Robin J. Williams, *American Society* (New York: Knopf, 1950), pp. 388-441.

13

See Franklin Frazier, *The Negro in the United States,* rev. ed. (New York: Macmillan, 1957), pp. 623-637, and his *Negro Family in the United States* (Chicago: University of Chicago Press, 1939).

14

A Treatise on Overpopulation Taken from Interviews, Sermons and Lectures of Father Divine (Philadelphia: New Day Publishing, 1967), p. 12.

15

Ibid., p. 11.

16

Ibid.

17

Ibid.

18

Ibid., p. 30.

19

Ibid., p. 10.

20

Ibid., p. 11.

21

W. I. Thomas, *The Unadjusted Girl* (New York: Social Science Research Council, 1923), p. 41.

22

W. I. Thomas, *Social Behavior and Personality,* ed. E. H. Volkart (New York: Social Science Research Council, 1951), p. 8.

23
Cf. Merton, *Social Theory,* ch. 11, "The Self-Fulfilling Prophecy."
24
Cf. Cohn, *Pursuit of the Millennium,* and Wallis, *Messiahs.*
25
Francis D. Nichol, *The Midnight Cry* (Washington, D.C.: Review and Herald Publishing, 1944).
26
Booton Herndon, *The Seventh Day* (New York: McGraw-Hill, 1960).
27
Wallis, *Messiahs*; cf. also Hans Kohn, "Messianism," *Encyclopedia of the Social Sciences,* vol. 10, pp. 356–363; A. H. Silver, *A History of Messianic Speculation in Israel* (Boston: Beacon Press, 1959).
28
New Day, March 9, 1968, p. 1.
29
Spoken June 24, 1938; *New Day,* March 9, 1968, p. 14

Bibliography

Andrews, Edward D. *The People Called Shakers*. New York: Oxford University Press, 1953.

Bendix, Reinhard. *Max Weber: An Intellectual Portrait*. Garden City: Doubleday, 1960.

Bierstedt, Robert. "An Analysis of Social Power," *American Sociological Review* 15:730–738, 1950.

Braden, Charles H. *Christian Science Today,* Dallas: Southern Methodist University Press, 1958.

Cantril, Hadley. *The Psychology of Social Movements*. New York: Wiley, 1944.

Crumb, C. B., Jr. "Father Divine's Use of Colloquial and Original English," *American Speech* 15:327, 1940.

Dohrman, H. T. *California Cult*. Boston: Beacon Press, 1958.

Doyle, Bertram. *The Etiquette of Race Relations in the South*. Chicago: University of Chicago Press, 1937.

Drake, St. Clair, and Cayton, Horace R. *Black Metropolis*. New York: Harcourt, Brace, 1945.

Durkheim, Emile. *The Elementary Forms of the Religious Life*. New York: Collier, 1961.

Eister, A. W. *Drawing Room Conversion: A Sociological Account of the Oxford Group Movement*. Durham: Duke University Press, 1950.

Fauset, Arthur Huff. *Black Gods of the Metropolis*. Philadelphia: University of Pennsylvania Press, 1944.

Festinger, Leon; Riecken, Henry W.; and Schachter, Stanley. *When Prophecy Fails*. Minneapolis: University of Minnesota Press, 1956.

Frazier, E. Franklin. *Black Bourgeoisie*. Glencoe: The Free Press, 1956.

————— *The Negro Family in the United States*. Chicago: University of Chicago Press, 1939.

———— *The Negro in the United States.* New York: Macmillan, 1957.

Gerstner, John H. *The Theology of the Major Sects.* Grand Rapids: Baker Book House, 1960.

Gerth, Hans, and Mills, C. W. *From Max Weber: Essays in Sociology.* New York: Oxford University Press, 1958.

Glock, Charles Y. "The Sociology of Religion." In *Sociology Today,* ed. Robert K. Merton. New York: Basic Books, 1959.

Harris, Sarah. *Father Divine: Holy Husband.* Garden City: Doubleday, 1953. Rev. ed., *Father Divine.* New York: Collier, 1971.

Hoshor, John. *God in a Rolls Royce: The Rise of Father Divine, Madman, Menace or Messiah.* New York: Hillman-Curl, 1936.

Hoult, Thomas Ford. *The Sociology of Religion.* New York: Dryden Press, 1958.

King, Wendell C. *Social Movements in the United States.* New York: Random House, 1956.

Liebling, A. J. "Who Is This King of Glory?" In *True Tales from the Annals of Crime and Rascality,* ed. St. Clair McKelway. New York: Random House, 1950.

Loescher, Frank. *The Protestant Church and the Negro.* New York: Association Press, 1948.

Melcher, Marguerite F. *The Shaker Adventure.* Cleveland: The Press of Western Reserve University, 1960.

Merton, Robert K. *Social Theory and Social Structure,* rev. ed. Glencoe: The Free Press, 1957.

Merton, Robert K., ed. *Sociology Today.* New York: Basic Books, 1959.

Mooney, James. *The Ghost Dance Religion and the Sioux Outbreak of 1890.* Washington, D.C.: United States Bureau of American Ethnology, Fourteenth Annual Report, part 2, 1896.

New Day. Weekly newspaper of the Peace Mission Movement, 1936–1978. Philadelphia: New Day Publishing Company.

Noyes, J. P. *My Father's House.* New York: Farrar, 1937.

O'Dea, Thomas. *The Mormons.* Chicago: University of Chicago Press, 1957.

Parker, Robert Allerton. *The Incredible Messiah: The Deification of Father Divine.* Boston: Little, Brown, 1937.

────── *Yankee Saint: John Humphrey Noyes and the Oneida Community.* New York: Putnam's, 1935.

Poll, Solomon. "The Economic Organization of a Religious Community," Ph.D. dissertation, University of Pennsylvania, 1961.

────── *The Hasidic Community of Williamsburg.* Glencoe: The Free Press, 1962.

Raper, Arthur F. *The Tragedy of Lynching.* Chapel Hill: University of North Carolina Press, 1933.

Rose, Arnold. *The Negro in America.* Boston: Beacon Press, 1944.

────── *The Negro's Morale.* Minneapolis: University of Minnesota Press, 1949.

Sklare, Marshall. *Conservative Judaism.* Glencoe: The Free Press, 1955.

Spero, Sterling D., and Harris, Abram L. *The Black Worker.* New York: Harper, 1931.

Sterner, Richard. *The Negro's Share.* New York: Harper, 1944.

Stroup, H. H. *Jehovah's Witnesses.* New York: Columbia University Press, 1945.

Thomas, W. I. *Primitive Behavior: An Introduction to the Social Sciences.* New York: McGraw-Hill, 1937.

United States Congressional Record. Vol. 83, part 1, January 1938.

Wallace, Anthony F. C. "Revitalization Movements." *American Anthropologist* 58:274 (April) 1956.

Wallis, Wilson D. *Messiahs: Christian and Pagan.* Boston: Richard G. Badger, 1918.

────── *Messiahs: Their Role in Civilization.* Washington, D.C.: Public Affairs Press, 1943.

Weaver, Robert C. *Negro Labor.* New York: Harcourt, Brace, 1946.

Weber, Max. *The Theory of Social and Economic Organization,* trans. A. M. Henderson and Talcott Parsons. New York: Oxford University Press, 1947.

Whitley, Oliver Read. *Trumpet Call of Reformation.* St. Louis: Bethany Press, 1949.

Who's Who. Chicago: A. N. Marquis, 1930.

Williams, Robin J. *American Society.* New York: Alfred A. Knopf, 1950.

Wilson, Bryan R. *Sects and Society.* Berkeley: University of California Press, 1961.

Yinger, J. Milton. *Religion, Society and the Individual.* New York: Macmillan, 1957.

Young, Pauline V. *The Pilgrims of Russian Town.* Chicago: University of Chicago Press, 1932.

Index